TEXAS TRAIN ROBBERIES

W. C. JAMESON

LONE
STAR
BOOKS

Guilford, Connecticut
Helena, Montana

LONE STAR BOOKS

An imprint of Globe Pequot
An imprint and registered trademark of Rowman & Littlefield

Distributed by NATIONAL BOOK NETWORK

Copyright © 2017 W. C. Jameson
Illustrations by Richard "Peewee" Kolb

British Library Cataloguing in Publication Information Available

Library of Congress Cataloging-in-Publication Data
Name: Jameson, W. C., 1942–, author.
Title: Texas train robberies / W. C. Jameson.
Description: Guilford, Connecticut : Lone Star Books, 2017. | Includes
    bibliographical references and index.
Identifiers: LCCN 2017027393 (print) | LCCN 2017026120 (ebook) |
    ISBN 9781493028665 (electronic) | ISBN 9781493028658 (pbk. : alk. paper)
Subjects: LCSH: Train robberies—Texas—History. | Brigands and robbers—
    Texas—History. | Texas—History—1846–1950. | Outlaws—Texas—History.
Classification: LCC F391 (print) | LCC F391 .J3563 2017 (ebook) |
    DDC 976.4/05—dc23
LC record available at https://lccn.loc.gov/2017027393

♾™ The paper used in this publication meets the minimum requirements of American National Standard for Information Sciences—Permanence of Paper for Printed Library Materials, ANSI/NISO Z39.48-1992.

CONTENTS

INTRODUCTION

Train robberies hold a dual fascination for multiple generations of Americans. First of all, children, as well as adults, are enchanted by trains and railroads. What child has not spent countless hours with a toy train or a model railroad? What youth has not thrilled at the sight and sound of a passing freight train at a railroad crossing?

This enchanted awe does not stop with age. Adults confess to experiencing the same kind of delight at the sight and sound of a large and powerful locomotive thundering down the tracks pulling dozens of cars filled with goods, fuel, or passengers. Tens of thousands of adults are involved with model railroading to the extent that national conferences and commercial publications are dedicated to the activity. Trains provide a number of elements many find enthralling: power, speed, sound, and more.

Second, not only have Americans long been fascinated with trains, but they, along with Europeans and Asians, feel a special attraction to and fondness for American outlaws, for the men and women who charted their own paths, followed their own rules, and flaunted authority. Studies have shown that while many Americans cannot name significant politicians, businessmen, and community leaders, they know well the names and exploits of colorful and adventurous outlaws such as Frank and Jesse James, Butch Cassidy, Sam Bass, "Black Jack" Ketchum, Rube and Jim Burrow, and the

Newton brothers. All of these individuals, incidentally, were notorious train robbers.

Train-robbing escapades have given rise to other famous outlaws. Among them Harvey Logan, Harry Longabaugh (the Sundance Kid), Elzy Lay, and Ben Kilpatrick were all, at one time or another, members of the notorious outlaw gang the Wild Bunch, who, along with Cassidy, were most famous for robbing trains. Add to this list outlaws such as George "Flat Nose" Currie, George "Big Nose" Parrott, the Dalton Gang, the Doolin Gang, the Sontag Brothers, Al Jennings, the Reno Gang, and more.

We love trains and we love outlaws, particularly train robbers. Although no train-robbing incidents have been reported for decades, the excitement and daring associated with this criminal activity have not dimmed. Novels are still written and movies are still made wherein train robbery is a significant part of the plot.

Without doubt, trains have played a prominent role in the history of the settlement and development of the United States. The railroads linked cities and towns of North America as they never had been before, transporting goods and people far more efficiently and effectively than did the wagon trains, stagecoaches, and waterways.

Expanding railroads represented a robust economy. A vast network of tracks was responsible for the transportation of goods and passengers across the country, along with payrolls and other diverse shipments of money, bonds, and notes, as well as gold and silver ingots. The railroads provided much-needed jobs. For a time, some of the wealthiest men in the United States were railroad magnates, including Jay and George Gould, Edward Harriman, James Hill, Collis P. Huntington, J. P. Morgan, and Cornelius Vanderbilt.

Just as prerailroad travelers, stagecoach lines, and banks attracted robbers, trains likewise held an appeal for those who earned their living taking money and valuables from others. Trains transported passengers, many of whom carried large sums of money along with items such as jewelry, watches, and more. And as noted, trains also transported large sums of cash and coin in express and mail cars, some in the form of payrolls. Gold and silver ingots often were transported from their point of origin to banks hundreds of miles away. When trains began to dominate the transportation landscape of America, some of them carrying rich cargo, they became obvious targets for banditti.

The first recorded train robbery in America took place on October 6, 1866, at Seymour, Indiana. The act appeared to have been carried off with relative ease and no doubt attracted the

Locations of train robberies in Texas

attention of other real and potential robbers. Not much time passed before similar activity began spreading along the Atlantic coast and through the West and the South.

On February 22, 1878, the first train robbery in Texas occurred in the small town of Allen, twenty-five miles north of Dallas. It marked the inauspicious beginning of a number of additional train robberies in the Lone Star State. Most attempts were carried out successfully, a few were thwarted, and some were marked with violence, leaving people injured or dead.

In addition to relieving passengers of their money and valuables, many train robbers soon began to focus on looting express and mail cars. Bandits learned quickly that these special cars transported, at times, great sums of money and other items of value. Cars or safes that the messengers traveling inside could or would not open were often dynamited. Misuse or poor placement of the charges sometimes resulted in the complete destruction of the car.

The train robbery era in Texas took place from 1878 to 1921, a period of forty-three years. During this time, fortunes were removed from express and mail cars as well as from passengers. Rarely were any of the stolen items recovered. Save for a few instances, most of the train robbers were never captured. Rarely during the course of a train robbery was the perpetrator killed.

Some train robberies caused damage in excess of tens of thousands of dollars due to derailed and toppled locomotives and cars, damaged tracks, dynamited mail and express cars, and more. In response, the railroad companies invested heavily in security measures, ranging from strengthening the express cars to hiring armed guards and private detectives.

One rarely reads or hears about train robbery anymore. Passengers carrying great sums of money are fewer these days, and most prefer traveling in their own vehicles. Money can be transported far more efficiently and effectively via other means. Thus, trains have become significantly less of a target for bandits than before.

The train robbery era of Texas is consigned to history, its time a century past. Like many historical periods, that associated with Texas train robberies remains exciting and was associated with notable, famous, and often colorful events and outlaw characters that have somehow never been removed from our consciousness.

SOME TRAIN ROBBERY TERMINOLOGY

Before we undertake a reading of the following Texas train robberies and robbers, a bit of explanation will acquaint the reader with specific items and jargon associated with railroad companies and with trains and their components.

BLIND

The blind was a walkway between two passenger cars. This space was generally open to the weather but sometimes covered with accordion-pleated leather or canvas. From the outside of the blinds to the outer edge of the cars was a space about twenty-four inches wide. A ladder ran from this space to the top of the car. Hobos would occasionally grab the ladder, climb a few rungs, and hold on to it. This practice was called "riding the blinds." Train robbers who wanted to board a train just as it was pulling away from the station would sometimes jump onto the blind and ride there until they were ready to make their way to the locomotive and force the engineer to stop the train.

BOILER

The boiler is a closed vessel found on steam engines in which water was heated. A boiler was sometimes referred to as a steam generator. During the early days of railroads when steam-powered locomotives were in use, trains made frequent stops between their point of origin and destination to take on water for the boiler and fuel for the coal tender.

COAL TENDER

A specialized rail car immediately behind the steam locomotive used to carry coal, a water supply, and tools is called the coal tender.

CONDUCTOR

A conductor is a railroad employee in charge of the train and its crew. On passenger trains, the conductor was also responsible for tasks such as assisting passengers and collecting tickets.

ENGINEER

The engineer is a railroad employee responsible for operating the locomotive.

EXPRESS CARS

The train vehicle that was designated an express car transported money, certificates, and other valuables. The first express cars were not designed to protect the contents from robbers since expectations of theft were low at the beginning. For the most part the cars were made of wood, the doors and sides easily pierced by bullets. The doors could be pried open with iron bars.

Oddly, the railroads and express companies were slow to respond to security concerns, and more fortified express cars did not come about for twenty years. In time, some of the cars were fitted with doors plated with iron, but most believed that such improvements were useless since any robber with a few sticks of dynamite could break into any car on the line. The railroad companies also were concerned with the expense associated with providing more bandit-resistant cars. Many companies believed that the rates associated with transporting items via express cars did not warrant the expense of bulletproofing and other improvements.

In addition to armoring and fortifying express cars, other modifications were made. Some of the cars had gun ports: slits cut in the side into which rifles could be inserted to defend against bandits. Some cars were equipped with Gatling guns, lanterns, and searchlights. Others were fitted with a steel cubicle at one end from which the messenger could theoretically hold off robbers with a rifle, should bandits gain access to the car.

One interesting and effective development came in the form of a hole in the floor of the express car into which a specially designed "iron cone" was inserted. While the robbers were milling about outside the car, the messenger could insert a shotgun into the cone. The cone would deflect the pellets, causing them to be sprayed laterally. Any bandits standing nearby could have their lower legs sprayed with buckshot.

In 1892, Wells Fargo and Company (WF & Co.) introduced a "reinforced" express car. While it proved slightly more resistant to robbers, it could, in fact, be breached easily with dynamite, which occurred on occasion. Dynamite, in fact, had destroyed numerous express cars over the years.

Because messengers responsible for the contents of the express cars rode inside in all kinds of weather, the vehicles were normally equipped with a potbellied stove and a supply of firewood to cope with freezing temperatures.

EXPRESS COMPANIES

As the railroads proliferated throughout the United States, it became clear to a number of businessmen, as well as government agencies, that trains represented a new and vastly improved manner in which to transport goods and cash. The express companies leased cars or car spaces from the railroads. Two of the first entrepreneurs to determine the value and utility of transporting goods and money via the railroads, and subsequently formalizing the practice, were brothers B. D. and L. B. Earle. Around 1835, the brothers formed Earle's Express Service, believed to be the first express service to use the railroads.

On the heels of the Earle brothers came William F. Harndon, who advanced the use and reputation of the express cars as an efficient way of transporting drafts, notes, currency, coin, and packages of all kinds of goods. Harndon, a former train conductor and ticket agent, was familiar with the operations of the railroads and was well connected in the business. Harndon also saw the value in advertising, and he ran ads in the Boston newspapers touting his business. He once stated that he would "run a car from Boston to New York [and back] four times a week." In a short time, he had all the trade he could handle, and his express business was well under way. Before long, almost every train had an express car. If business was good, some trains accommodated two.

As the railroads expanded, so did the real and perceived need for express companies and express cars. Railroads around the country lost no time in entering into extended business agreements with express companies.

In 1839, the Adams Express Company was established by Alvin Adams. In 1845, the company signed a contract with the New York and New Haven Railroad, paying $1,000 per car pulled by the trains, an amount deemed rather exorbitant at the time. Rapid growth followed, however, and the Adams Express Company soon had hundreds of employees, most of them working twelve hours per day. By the end of the 1850s, the Adams Express Company handled most of the express business along the Eastern Seaboard.

As train robberies occurred with greater frequency, the Adams Express Company hired armed guards to accompany shipments, along with detectives to assist in determining who was responsible for the theft of merchandise and money. If necessary, they were sometimes called on to track down and apprehend the robbers. It was the first company to do so. One of its first contracts was with Allan Pinkerton, who went on to found the Pinkerton National Detective Agency. Some of the first men taken into custody and questioned relative to theft of money and merchandise turned out to be Adams Express Company employees.

In 1850, the American Express Company (AEC) was established in Buffalo, New York, to handle shipments for the Hudson River Railroad. Not long after, the company secured additional contracts with other major railroad companies throughout the East and Midwest. The American Express Company also handled shipments of money and goods via steamboats, which traveled up and down the East Coast, via a network of inland canals, and into the Great Lakes. By 1858, the AEC was covering most of the midwestern states and transporting over $2 million per day. By 1862, AEC had nearly nine hundred offices in ten states and over fifteen hundred full-time employees.

Engine, coal tender, and express car

In 1867, the Merchant Union Express Company was formed in New York City and offered serious competition to the AEC. The two companies eventually merged into the American Merchants Union Express Company. By 1882, it had gone back to being the American Express Company. By the 1890s, the company was issuing American Express Travelers Cheques.

As the potential for Civil War loomed over the nation during the late 1850s, many expressed concern that all northern businesses operating in the American South would be confiscated. Anticipating this, Henry B. Plant, who was in charge of the southern division of the Adams Express Company, suggested that it be sold to him. Plant implied that if it were not, he would simply start a company of his own and take over all the Adams routes. An agreement was reached, and the Southern Express Company was formed. It soon took over all the express business related to Alabama, Arkansas, North and South Carolina, Georgia, Florida, Louisiana, Mississippi, Tennessee, Texas, and Virginia. Following the war, the Southern Express Company fell on hard times due to the deteriorated economic conditions throughout much of the South.

In 1852, Wells Fargo and Company organized to take advantage of the growing express business in California, which was experiencing a mining boom at the time. A number of the founders of the WF & Co. had previously been associated with the American Express Company. The company not only shipped freight coast to coast but also engaged in the purchase and sale of gold. Much of this gold was transported by stagecoaches until the railroads became established.

It was not long before WF & Co. became a major player in the freighting business, with mail contracts and stagecoach lines. Eventually, most of the WF & Co. shipping business was transferred to the railroads. The company aligned itself primarily with the Central Pacific and Southern Pacific railroads. By 1880, WF & Co. had 2,830 agencies spread across the country. It was also the only transport company that could move goods into and out of California. Between 1855 and 1917, WF & Co. was regarded as the preeminent express company in the American West. As a result of its success, WF & Co.'s money and goods-laden cars became targets for enterprising train robbers, whom the company had to deal with for nearly half a century.

EXPRESS COMPANY SAFES

Attention was not limited to strengthening express cars in the hope of discouraging robbers. During the 1890s, the express companies applied some effort to developing safes that would prove more difficult and time-consuming to open. Since it was in the best interest of the train robber to conduct the heist quickly and efficiently, a near-impenetrable safe could disrupt the process. In time, safes were developed that proved nearly dynamite-proof, but they were expensive. Some railroad companies opted not to purchase them, often to their regret.

Even with the development of armored railroad cars and so-called dynamite-proof safes, the evidence suggests that those measures were not as effective in discouraging robberies as the railroad and express companies initially believed. Robberies declined noticeably only when it became common knowledge that the express companies were transporting less money. It became less expensive and more efficient to ship money and other valuables by registered mail via alternative carriers.

EXPRESS MESSENGERS

Express cars were generally accompanied by at least one messenger and sometimes as many as three. The term "messenger" as applied by the railroads meant "courier." The messenger traveled in the express car, maintained the paperwork associated with what was being transported, and was, to a large degree, responsible for everything in the car. That is why most messengers were so resistant to intrusion from robbers, often refusing to open the express car door even under threat of death. Messengers often lost their jobs when their car had been robbed.

FIREBOX

With steam-powered locomotives, the firebox was a chamber that provided heat sufficient to create steam once the hot gases from the firebox were carried into the adjacent boiler via tubes or flues.

FIREMAN

The railroad fireman was a member of the train crew who shoveled coal into the furnace and tended the boiler on steam locomotives. His job was to make certain that the train had the power necessary to negotiate hills and turns.

MAIL CARS

Mail cars were similar to, but separate from, express cars. Contracts related to transporting the US mail were also similar to, but entirely separate from, express deliveries. On rare occasions, small mail and express deliveries were combined in one car.

Because of the increasing robberies of mail cars, the US Postal Service decided to do something. At first, it considered procuring armored cars for its railway operations but in the end opted to strengthen existing cars. After a 1924 robbery of a Chicago, Milwaukee, and St. Paul train at Rondout, Illinois, in which at least $2 million and perhaps as much as $4 million was taken, the Postal Service ordered bullet- and gas-proof armored cars. This new postal car also boasted bulletproof windows, gun ports through which rifles could be fired at bandits, and two specially designed holes through which flares could be fired during night-time robberies to illuminate the area.

PINKERTON NATIONAL DETECTIVE AGENCY

Founded in 1855 by Allan Pinkerton, this agency worked closely with midwestern railroads. Pinkerton duties included investigating theft of property as well as dealing with labor problems and customer complaints. Because the Pinkerton agents were not affiliated with the US government, they were not subject to federal rules and regulations. The agency was often criticized for unorthodox methods related to pursuing and capturing train robbers, but in the end the railroad companies were satisfied with their efforts. Real and potential train robbers had reason to be apprehensive of the persistent Pinkertons.

RAILROAD POLICE

By the 1870s a number of railroads had become so impressed with the effectiveness of the Pinkerton National Detective Agency that they decided to establish their own police and security forces. While express messengers and postal and baggage clerks were responsible for the contents of their respective cars, the railroad police provided a modicum of security. More often than not, they were involved with tracking down and apprehending robbers. Members of the railroad police were referred to as "detectives."

Railroad police generally were armed with a handgun and club and issued a badge from the company. However, few of them had any formal training as detectives or, for that matter, in any kind of police procedure. Their methods were often bullying and brutal, and the railroad police were looked down upon by legitimate law enforcement officers.

TRESTLE

A trestle is a style of bridge over a gully, river, or any other type of gorge for roads or railroads. It consists of a braced framework of wood or metal.

CHAPTER 1

SAM BASS, TEXAS'S FIRST TRAIN ROBBER

Sam Bass was born into a large family on a farm near Mitchell in southern Indiana on July 21, 1851. (At least one writer gives the date as July 2, 1851.) When he was but a small child, Sam's mother passed away. An older brother who enlisted in the Union Army was killed at the Battle of Richmond in 1862. Sam, along with his siblings, pitched in and helped his father with the hard work and long hours associated with farming. By all accounts, the farm prospered.

When his father died in 1864, Sam went to live with his uncle, Dave Sheeks. Sheeks was regarded by his neighbors as wealthy and owned a number of large farms and sawmills in the vicinity. During his time in Indiana, Bass never received any education. He was able to read only a few words and was barely able to sign his name. While he was a hard and dependable worker, farming held little appeal to the young Bass, and he began making plans to head out west at the first opportunity.

While growing up, Bass heard stories about the Reno Gang, a band of bank, stagecoach, and train robbers who operated through-out much of Indiana and Illinois. The Reno Gang is credited with the first peacetime robbery of a train on October 6, 1866, in Seymour, Indiana, forty miles northeast of Mitchell. The robbers, holding the express car messenger at gunpoint, took $12,000 from the safe and got away with no difficulty. (One account estimates that $90,000 was taken in the heist.) An escapade such as this appeared to offer far more adventure and excitement, not to mention income, than young Sam was experiencing on the farm.

From travelers who stopped at the Sheeks farms, Bass heard stories of the American West, stories of cowboys, buffalo hunters, and Indian fighters. He was known to have expressed a desire to journey westward to see for himself what adventures might lie there. It was said that he once mentioned to an acquaintance that he might take up robbing trains like the Reno Gang.

Bass left home at around eighteen years of age. One of his first stops was Rosedale, Mississippi. In need of money, he found work as a farm laborer for a time.

While in Rosedale, according to one biographer, Bass learned to shoot a gun and play cards. By all accounts, he was a decent shot with a revolver but a terrible poker player.

From Rosedale Bass traveled to Arkansas, then on to northern Texas, hitching a ride with a family traveling in a covered wagon, eventually arriving in Denton County some time in 1870. He had no trouble finding employment on nearby ranches. His commitment to his tasks impressed those around him, and he was regarded by all who knew him as responsible and frugal. As with farming, Bass soon learned that he had no love for working on ranches.

Bass left the ranch work and went to live in the town of Denton. He found work at times as a stable boy, a handyman, and a freight wagon driver.

By the time he was an adult, Sam Bass was five feet, six inches tall. He had grown lean and muscular from hard work. His posture was a bit stooped, which gave the impression that he was much older. With his black hair and deep black eyes, he was often mistaken for an Indian. According to researchers, Bass was somewhat careless in his personal appearance; it was said he seldom bathed or shaved except when posing for the rare photograph.

Bass's biographers have written that he rarely showed any interest in female company. As far as is known, Bass was never romantically or otherwise linked with a woman during his lifetime.

One of Bass's interests was horses, and he grew adept at raising, training, and breeding them. His desire was to generate a stock of good racing horses, and in time he developed into a skillful breeder. Whenever Bass had the opportunity, he traveled around the countryside entering his animals in racing competitions. In addition to Denton, he raced in Dallas, Fort Worth, Grandbury, Waco, San Antonio, and other locations in Texas as well as in Oklahoma. He won more than he lost. When not racing his horses, Bass spent his time drinking and gambling.

Sam Bass

During his time of raising and racing horses, Bass found himself in trouble with the law on occasion. In one case he was charged with doping his horses. In another, he was alleged to have cheated an opponent out of a race by intimidating the judges.

After a few weeks of racing his famed Denton mare in San Antonio, Bass fell in with a man named Joel Collins. Collins was a former saloon owner who spent a lot of his time at the horse races. Like Bass, Collins had had a few scrapes with the law. He was described as a "violent, reckless man who had killed a Mexican or two."

In 1876, Bass and Collins, along with three other cowhands, drove a herd of cattle to Dodge City, Kansas, where they attempted to sell it. By the time they had arrived in Dodge City, the herd was considerably larger than when they left Texas, leading biographers to speculate that more cattle were obtained along the trail by theft. Questions of ownership arose that Bass and Collins were unable to answer satisfactorily, negating the possibilities of a sale. In response to the growing suspicions, they moved the herd northward to Nebraska, where it was finally sold. After paying off the cowhands, Bass and Collins pocketed $8,000.

From Nebraska, Bass and Collins traveled northward into Dakota Territory, landing in the town of Deadwood. There, they invested their money in a freight company, a zinc mine, and a whorehouse. Between the hard drinking and compulsive gambling, neither Bass nor Collins could focus on their enterprises long enough to make a go of them, and eventually they all folded.

Following one business failure after another, the two men met Jack Davis, a fellow gambler. Davis, who had experience robbing stagecoaches, pointed out that they were used to transport shipments of gold from the mines. To the three men, robbing stages seemed like an easier way to make a living. A handful of additional men were added to the gang, and plans were made to rob a coach. So broke were Bass, Collins, and the others that they had to steal horses and saddles in order to perpetrate the holdup.

For Bass and Collins, the occasional stagecoach robbery kept them in money, and the money kept them in alcohol and at the gaming tables. This was not to last, however, for the area law enforcement, seeking to put a stop to the holdups, was closing in. Enraged by the killing of a stagecoach driver during one of the robberies, lawmen were determined to end the reign of terror along the roads and to bring the criminals to justice. Sensing this, Bass and Collins, along with gang members Jack Davis, Jim Berry, Tom Nixon, and Bill Heffridge, decided it was time to leave the Dakotas and travel south. Along the way, they made plans to rob a Union Pacific train.

On the evening of September 1877, Sam Bass and his gang robbed the Union Pacific train at the tiny community of Big Springs, twenty miles west of Ogallala in western Nebraska. The Big Springs train robbery ushered in Bass's short but effective and colorful career as a train robber.

At gunpoint, Bass and five companions entered the station and secured it, taking the stationmaster prisoner. Moments later, the outlaws cut the telegraph lines. They forced the stationmaster to stand beside the tracks and wave a red lantern, a signal to the engineer of the arriving train to pull to a stop.

Within an hour the scheduled train arrived and chugged to a halt. The outlaws entered the cab of the locomotive and neutralized the engineer and fireman. They doused the firebox with water so the train could not proceed. Following this, Bass and Collins walked down the tracks, identified the express car, and broke into it with little difficulty. Moments later, the train robbers made their getaway with $60,000 in twenty-dollar gold pieces, all fresh from the San Francisco mint, along with $500 in currency. Before departing, one of the gang members pistol-whipped the freight agent.

The six outlaws rode away from the holdup eager to spend their newfound riches. At the time, it represented the biggest haul from a train robbery in history.

After fleeing the scene of the robbery, some of the gang members talked about the advantages of traveling to South America, then a popular destination for American outlaws who were feeling the law close in on them. There was little agreement to this plan, and the gang members decided to split up. Joel Collins and Bill Heffridge rode away to Kansas. Jim Berry and Tom Nixon traveled to Kansas City, Missouri. Sam Bass, accompanied by Jack Davis, headed for Texas.

Initially, law enforcement authorities believed the Big Springs train had been robbed by the Jesse James Gang, which by this time had gained a major reputation for such activities. Following an intense investigation, it was later determined the holdup had been perpetrated by a gang consisting of Bass, Collins, and four other men.

Not long after arriving in Kansas, Collins and Heffridge made plans to rob a Kansas Pacific Railroad train at Buffalo Station in the west-central part of the state. On their way to the station, the two outlaws encountered a squad of soldiers from Fort Hays. Riding with the troopers were several area law enforcement authorities who became suspicious of the two men. A shootout ensued, and both Collins and Heffridge were killed.

On arriving in Denton County, Texas, Bass spotted his likeness on wanted posters along with a description of his role in the Nebraska train robbery. He decided to lay low for a time, hiding out in a remote region in the northwestern corner of the county called Cove Hollow, an area with which he was already familiar.

Bass found comfort in being back in Texas. With a reward out for him, however, he realized it would be difficult to return to raising and training horses. He decided the best way to make a living was to pursue something else he was good at: train robbery. To Sam Bass, the growing and expanding railroad businesses in Texas offered a vast array of opportunities.

CHAPTER 2

ALLEN, TEXAS

February 22, 1878

Emboldened by the successful Big Springs, Nebraska, train robbery, Bass lost little time in putting together another gang to perpetrate more. He recruited Frank "Blockey" Jackson, Seaborn Barnes, and Tom Spotswood. Other gang members who came and went during Bass's time in Texas included Henry Underwood, Arkansas Johnson, Jim Murphy, Pipes Herndon, and William Collins, a cousin of Joel Collins.

While studying his chances of pulling off another train robbery, Bass learned about shipments of payrolls and other monies by stagecoaches traveling into and out of Fort Worth, several miles to the south. After two successful coach holdups but without much to show for the effort, Bass once again turned his sights toward the railroads, redoubling his efforts to determine a suitable target. And he found it.

The February 22, 1878, robbery of the Houston and Texas Central (H&TC) passenger train in Allen, Texas, was notable for two principle reasons: it was the first recorded train robbery in the state of Texas, and it was organized and carried out by a man who would become one of Texas's most famous outlaws, Sam Bass. In fact, it was the first of four train robberies Bass was to commit in Texas before he met his end at the hands of Texas Rangers several months later.

In mid-February 1878, Bass and his gang rode into Allen, located in Collin County, twenty-five miles north-northeast of downtown Dallas. From a hiding place in a nearby clump of trees, the outlaws observed the comings and goings of the H&TC trains and the activities of employees at the station. Built in 1872, the H&TC was purchased by J. P. Morgan in 1877. As they watched, the gang members learned the arrival and departure times of the trains and the shifts and schedules of the station employees. Bass explained to his gang members how they were going to execute the robbery of the train.

On the afternoon of February 22, just a few minutes before the arrival of an H&TC train, Bass and his gang stormed into the station and subdued the agent, the lone person on duty.

The oncoming H&TC train was not scheduled to stop, but Bass ordered the agent to alert the engineer to make certain that it did. The agent offered no resistance. Once the train was flagged down, James Thomas, the express messenger, opened the express car door to ascertain the reason. When he spotted what he took to be robbers approaching the Texas Express company car, Thomas retrieved his revolver and fired several shots at them. The gang immediately returned fire, but no one was hit. Thomas scrambled back into the express car and locked the door.

When Bass finally arrived at the express car, he pounded on the door and demanded that it be opened. Inside the car, messenger Thomas took refuge behind some wooden trunks and prepared to resist the bandits.

As Bass carried on a dialog with Thomas, another gang member raced through the passenger cars shouting that a robbery was taking place and that fifty to sixty outlaws were involved. His intention was to force the passengers to seek cover and not leave the train. No one did. Bass had earlier decided not to rob or harm the passengers.

Meanwhile, back at the express car, Thomas continued to refuse to open the door. The outlaws fired their revolvers into the car, and Thomas fired back. Thomas was slightly wounded by one of the outlaw's bullets. After a few minutes, out of ammunition and concerned about his bleeding wound, Thomas surrendered and opened the door. After the outlaws climbed into the express car, Bass ordered Thomas to open the safe. The messenger refused, but when Bass threatened to kill him if he didn't, he complied. From the safe, Bass removed, according to some documents, between $1,200 and $2,500. At least one other report, however, suggested that the outlaws got away with less than $500.

Moments later, with Bass in the lead, the gang mounted their horses and rode away toward their Cove Hollow hideout. The robbery had gone off with little difficulty. None of the passengers were harmed, and express messenger Thomas's wound was minor.

Two days following the Allen train robbery, hundreds of wanted posters appeared throughout the region with offers of a $1,500 reward for the capture of each of the train robbers. Gang member Tom Spotswood, whose mask had fallen from his face during the robbery, was identified by messenger Thomas and arrested. Spotswood spent two years in jail while his case was in and out of the courts. He was finally acquitted.

Sam Bass and his gang retreated to the Cove Hollow hideout where they remained out of sight for several weeks. The outlaws spent their time playing cards. Encouraged by his success and the ease with which the Allen, Texas, holdup was accomplished, Sam Bass immediately began making plans for his next train robbery. It was to take place just over three and a half weeks later in Hutchins, Texas.

Local sheriff departments directed some of their attention to train schedules and kept themselves informed of valuable shipments. The Texas Rangers began to take an interest in Sam Bass and his gang of train robbers. Not much more time would pass before these two entities collided with one another.

CHAPTER 3

HUTCHINS, TEXAS

March 18, 1878

Sam Bass had grown convinced that robbing trains was an effective and efficient way to make a living. Thus far in his life, save for some horse-racing victories, train robbery was the only thing he'd ever had success with and that appealed to his oft-stated craving for adventure. He wanted to match the excitement of his Big Springs, Nebraska, holdup, and he longed to ride away with a similarly impressive amount of loot. To Sam Bass, train robbery was certainly easier and more lucrative than farming and ranching, and it provided for greater excitement. Convinced that he could outsmart and elude pursuit by area lawmen with little difficulty, the outlaw wasted no time in planning another holdup.

Bass determined that the chances for success were greater by conducting the robberies at small-town train stations. There would be fewer witnesses, the stations were generally manned by only one employee at a time, and law enforcement was negligible to nonexistent. Since robbing trains was unheard of in Texas until the incident with the Union Pacific train at Allen less than a month earlier, Bass knew well that lawmen were unprepared for such events and unpracticed in pursuit. After familiarizing himself with potential targets and train schedules, Bass decided to pull his next job at Hutchins, a tiny community ten miles southeast of Dallas.

According to information gleaned by Bass, the Houston and Texas Central Railroad's No. 4 train would arrive at the Hutchins station at 10:00 p.m. on March 18, 1878. Following the procedure established during the Big Springs robbery as well as the recent heist in Allen, Bass and his gang burst into the Hutchins station with guns drawn. The surprised and frightened stationmaster was tied up and placed in a closet. Minutes before the train arrived, the outlaws assembled on the depot loading platform.

After the H&TC No. 4 pulled to a stop at around 10:00 p.m., Bass led his companions to the locomotive and climbed into the cab. At gunpoint he and Frank Jackson ordered the engineer and fireman to raise their hands and step out onto the dock. As Bass busied himself questioning the engineer about what sort of monies were being transported in the express car, Texas Express Company agent Heck Thomas opened the car door and stepped down to the

Heck Thomas

ground. He was joined by the mail car clerk, a man named Terrell. As the two men engaged in conversation, they looked up and spotted the engineer and fireman with raised hands and immediately deduced that a robbery was underway. Scrambling back into the express car, Thomas began collecting the canvas bags containing money and searching for a suitable hiding place. In the end, he crammed the bags, containing $4,000, into the large potbellied stove and stovepipe. Terrell raced to the nearby mail car and did his best to hide what he determined were valuable shipments.

Moments later, Bass and his gang arrived at the express car and instructed Thomas to hand over the money bags. Thomas resisted, shots were fired, and the agent sustained bullet wounds to the face and neck.

During the confrontation at the express car, the train conductor, accompanied by the brakeman, ran through the passenger coaches warning of the robbery taking place and enlisting help from any of the male passengers who were armed. Several men gathered at the coach windows, lowered them, and began firing at the outlaws standing outside the express car, forcing them to take shelter.

Frustrated, Bass threatened to shoot the fireman if Thomas did not turn over the money. The agent surrendered and complied, handing over to Bass an amount of money that he had earlier set aside from the larger bags of cash. With a portion of the loot in hand and no indication that they would acquire any more, Bass and his gang, still being harassed by the shooting from the passengers, decided to forego an attempt on the mail car and beat a hasty retreat. Making their way back to the horses, they mounted up and rode away.

Bass led his men eastward. A posse of several volunteers was quickly put together and set off in pursuit of the outlaws. After riding hard for two miles, Bass and his gang arrived at the banks of the Trinity River. Without pausing, they turned north and headed for the Cove Hollow hideout in Denton County. The posse tracked the gang to the river but lost their trail a short time later. Following a fruitless effort to pick it back up, they decided to return to Hutchins.

Sam Bass was frustrated and disappointed with the haul from the H&TC No. 4 train. It amounted to far less than the take from the Allen train robbery. Most estimates suggest that the gang made off with only $500, but one report placed the amount at a mere $89.

Rather than linger on this discouraging development, Bass regarded the botched Hutchins train robbery as a fluke, the result of bad luck and no fault of his own. More than ever, he was convinced that robbing trains was the quickest and easiest path to wealth, and he began making plans to undertake another holdup as soon as possible. He set his sights on Eagle Ford, Texas.

· · ·

Addendum: Texas Express company agent Heck Thomas later became a significant western personality and ended up with a career in law enforcement. Having fought for the South during the Civil War, Thomas migrated west, settling in Texas, where he found work with the railroads. In time, he became a US deputy marshal stationed at Fort Smith, Arkansas, serving under US district judge Isaac C. Parker, the notorious "hanging judge." Working with other lawmen such as Bill Tilghman and Chris Madsen, Thomas has been largely credited with bringing law and order to Indian Territory, later Oklahoma. Thomas gained fame as an effective man hunter. In 1896, he tracked down and killed the notorious outlaw and train robber Bill Doolin.

CHAPTER 4

EAGLE FORD, TEXAS
April 4, 1878

With the passage of just over two weeks since his last train robbery, Sam Bass decided it was time to try another. For his next undertaking, he and his gang targeted the Texas and Pacific (T&P) Railroad and decided to hold it up when it arrived at midnight at the Eagle Ford station on April 4. Eagle Ford was located six miles west of downtown Dallas. After making their plans, the gang left their Denton County hideout in Cove Hollow and, traveling along back roads to avoid being seen by lawmen, made their way to the small community.

Bass was confident in his method but apparently suffered from a bit of complacency. He had little respect or regard for the railroads or, for that matter, law enforcement. He was convinced he was smarter and tougher than all of them and perceived them as only a minor and easily overcome obstacle to his goals. Bass's attitude and overconfidence were soon to cause some difficulties.

Unknown to Bass, the railroads and the express companies were developing strategies to deal with robbers and robberies. Since express cars were the obvious targets of the bandits, the companies decided on alternatives. One method developed to foil the bandits was to place money in bags carried by an agent or agents who traveled as passengers and rode in the coaches. In the case of the T&P train set to arrive at the Eagle Ford station, the agent was

15

a woman. In the past, the Sam Bass Gang had never bothered the passengers and remained particularly deferential to women.

The robbery was routine and followed the pattern of the previous two. The outlaw gang—composed of Bass, Arkansas Johnson, Seaborn Barnes, and one other unidentified man—met with little to no resistance from the stationmaster or the express company messenger and guard. After breaching the express car, the outlaws were simply handed a small bag containing some money by the frightened and timid express messenger. No shots were fired during the entire time. When the express company later learned that the messenger and guard had offered no resistance whatsoever to the outlaws, it terminated them.

After Bass and his gang had ridden what they perceived to be a safe distance from the robbery site, they stopped to camp for the night. After counting the money and finding it to consist of only a handful of bills, Bass began to suspect that they had been duped. He saw that he had been led to believe that he had conducted a successful robbery and had gotten away with it when, in truth, the bulk of the money shipment had been concealed elsewhere. Bass realized that he had escaped with only a token amount of money and that he and his gang were victims of a ruse, one perpetrated by either the railroad or the express company. Try as he might, he was at a loss to make sense of how it had happened.

Following the unsuccessful robbery, the outlaws once again mounted up and returned to the Denton County hideout. More than ever, Sam Bass was determined to make a big haul from a train robbery and began planning his next one, the sooner the better. He vowed to be more alert the next time.

CHAPTER 5

MESQUITE, TEXAS
April 10, 1878

Sam Bass's fourth train robbery in less than three months was not long in coming. With the Eagle Ford holdup still fresh in the minds of the outlaws, the railroad companies, the express companies, and area law enforcement personnel, the bold bandits decided to strike again. This time, they targeted a Texas and Pacific passenger train. Bass determined that the ideal location for the robbery would be Mesquite, Texas.

Mesquite offered a considerably different situation than the three previous robberies. Unlike the other small communities in which the holdups had been conducted, Mesquite was a sizeable town twelve miles east of downtown Dallas and boasted numerous residences, a general store, a blacksmith, churches, schools, and saloons.

The Sam Bass Gang, now consisting of Seaborn Barnes, Albert Herndon, Frank Jackson, Arkansas Johnson, Sam Pipes, Henry Underwood, and another unidentified man, all armed and masked, burst into the train station, subdued the agent, and trussed him up. This done, the gang members sat down to await the arrival of the T&P.

To this point, Bass's approach to robbing trains had followed a pattern that had proven successful. Thus far, the heists had all worked according to plan, and the outlaw saw no reason to change. On this attempt, however, Bass and his gang were to encounter more resistance than during previous ones, resistance for which they were unprepared.

When the train finally arrived, Frank Jackson entered the locomotive cab and held the engineer and fireman at gunpoint. A moment later, he ordered them to step out onto the platform. As Bass led the rest of the gang toward the express car, he did not reckon on the messenger, J. S. Kerley.

When the train had stopped, Kerley had opened the express car door and was preparing to drop off a package when he discerned that a robbery was about to take place. As the outlaws approached the express car, Kerley produced a handgun and opened fire on them. Though no one was struck, Bass and his gang members ducked for cover.

While Bass was deciding what to do next, Kerley used the opportunity to slam the express car door shut and lock it. Inside with Kerley were two guards, both armed. Reloading his handgun, the messenger took up a defensive position and prepared to protect the shipment from the bandits. While he was waiting for events to unfold, Kerley decided to hide the money. He stuffed canvas bags filled with bills and coin into the express car's stovepipe and pot-bellied stove. One estimate had the shipment at $1,500, but some reports claimed the train was carrying more than $30,000.

Bass and his gang were not prepared for resistance from the messenger. They likewise were startled by the intrusion of the T&P conductor, a Civil War veteran named Julius Alvord. On spotting Bass and his compatriots moving toward the express car, Alvord pulled a Derringer from his pocket and began firing at them from a passenger car. The Derringer had little effect other than amusing the outlaws. Alvord threw down the Derringer, secured a revolver, and began shooting anew. One of the outlaws responded by returning fire and subsequently wounding the conductor in the shoulder. Cursing the shooter, Alvord tossed away his weapon, climbed down from the coach, and marched into town screaming for a doctor to come and tend to his wound.

The outlaws also came under fire from the baggage clerk, B. F. Caperton. Caperton pulled a shotgun from a large canvas pack, slid the baggage car door open a few inches, and fired away, forcing the robbers to seek cover anew. Added to this, a youth selling newspapers and candy in the passenger car secured a revolver and also began firing at the outlaws. Bass called out to the boy, admonishing him not to interfere, and sent him away.

In order to remove themselves from the line of fire, the engineer and fireman dashed from the platform and took refuge beneath a nearby trestle. From this point, they watched the goings-on in relative safety.

Around the same time, new opposition to the train robbers appeared from yet another direction. On a siding not far away perched a special car filled with prison convicts assigned to construction labor. Accompanying the prisoners was a contingent of guards, all heavily armed. After observing the activity near the express car of the recently arrived T&P train, the guards opened fire on Bass and his gang of train robbers. Albert Herndon was hit in both legs and went down in great pain. Sam Pipes was struck in the side.

Apparently deciding not to use up all their ammunition on the train robbers and thereby provide the convicts an opportunity to take advantage, the guards ceased firing after only a few minutes.

Frustrated at not gaining access to the express car, Bass ran back to the locomotive and procured a can of kerosene. Though fired upon from different directions, he made it back to the car and pushed the can of kerosene through a narrow opening in the door. He shouted to the men inside that he was going to set the entire car afire if they did not surrender at once and come out. At first, the occupants of the car refused to budge, but when Bass doused the wooden door with the liquid and they heard him strike a match, they quickly agreed to throw down their weapons and vacate the express car.

More apparent resistance to the train robbers was about to materialize. As the occupants of the express car climbed to the ground, a local storekeeper arrived on the scene brandishing a pistol. He spotted the fireman hiding behind the trestle and, mistaking him for Sam Bass, forced him from his place of concealment at gunpoint. This done, the storekeeper announced to everyone within hearing distance that he had captured Sam Bass. Laughter immediately broke out, mostly among the outlaws, with none laughing as hard as Bass himself.

With the express car vacated, Bass and the others climbed in only to find themselves unable to locate the money bags. By the time Bass decided it was time to effect an escape, they had accumulated less than $200.

Leaving the express car, Bass and his companions helped the wounded Herndon and Pipes onto their horses. As the two bleeding men were secured in their saddles, the express messenger approached Bass and asked the outlaw leader to write out a receipt for the money he had taken from the express car. Ignoring the messenger, Bass mounted up and, leading his men, rode away.

The wounded Pipes and Herndon did not accompany the rest of the gang to the hideout in Denton County. Instead, they were dropped off at the farm of some friends outside Dallas, where they planned to rest and recuperate.

A few days later, however, Captain June Peak, leading a contingent of Texas Rangers, arrived at the farm and arrested the two outlaws. Peak had been tracking the train robbers since only a few hours after the robbery. Pipes and Herndon were charged with mail robbery, a federal crime. They were transported to Tyler, Texas, and locked in the city jail to await trial.

On April 8, Captain Peak and a squad of some thirty Texas Rangers arrived in Denton with warrants for Bass and other members of the gang. Denton sheriff Eagan also deputized several local citizens, and together the lawmen traveled to Cove Hollow in search of Bass and his gang. Once the lawmen arrived, shots were exchanged, and the outlaws fled deeper into the woods.

After reporting four train robberies within two months, area newspapers were filled with articles that spoke of the growing menace of outlaws. Walter Prescott Webb wrote that the train robberies "furnished the state more exciting news than it had known since Lee surrendered." Fearing a plague of outlawry, businessmen, bankers, and travelers armed themselves or placed weapons where they could be conveniently retrieved in case of an emergency.

Throughout the northern Texas region, passenger fares were down, with travelers expressing fear that they would be robbed. Businesses and banks, not trusting the abilities of the express companies and US mail, looked for alternative ways to send money and bonds. Private detectives and bounty hunters arrived in Dallas offering their services to go after the train robbers. US Marshal Stillwell H. Russell was put up at a Dallas hotel along with nineteen special deputies. Pinkerton detectives swarmed throughout Denton and Dallas counties in search of Sam Bass and his gang. The governor of Texas sent Major John B. Jones and a company of Texas Rangers to Dallas to investigate the robberies. A rumor spread that the Sam Bass Gang numbered eighty men. Rewards in excess of $8,000 were posted.

Warrants for Sam Bass, Seaborn Barnes, Frank Jackson, Arkansas Johnson, and Henry Underwood were issued. For the next several weeks, Sam Bass and his gang remained on the run, mostly hiding out in Cove Hollow. While Bass himself may have had a yearning to attempt more train robberies, he was now occupied with surviving and staying ahead of the law. With the expanding and intensified pursuit from Texas Rangers and other lawmen, it was beginning to look like Bass was running a race he would eventually lose.

CHAPTER 6

THE END OF SAM BASS
July 18, 1878

From his first Texas train robbery in Allen to his last in Mesquite, Sam Bass had gone from a mere suspect to a wanted outlaw, one now pursued across a great swath of the state. The railroads and express companies began applying pressure to area, state, and federal law enforcement agencies, and before long wanted posters on Bass and his gang were tacked up throughout much of the northern and central Texas region. Bass and his gang were constantly on the run, and lawmen were closing in.

Throughout the spring and summer of 1878, the Sam Bass Gang remained just out of reach of pursuing posses, taking refuge in the Cove Hollow hideout not far from where their leader had spent several years of his young adulthood. After a time, the gang fled from the hideout in northwestern Denton County and made their way along back roads into the wooded and marshy Hickory Creek region in the secluded southern part of the county. Even with the Texas Rangers and local sheriff's posse nipping at their heels, the gang would manage to rob a stagecoach now and then, efforts that kept them in enough money to purchase supplies and ammunition.

At times, the pursuing lawmen grew close enough to engage the outlaws in gun battle. During one encounter at the Warner Jackson farm near Bullard's Mill, a few miles north of the city of

Denton, three of the gang members suffered wounds but were able to ride away. The following morning, they rode into the small town of Bolivar, where they purchased fresh horses, new clothes, a supply of food, and several boxes of cartridges.

On June 13, Bass and his men were camped at Salt Creek in Wise County, about twenty-five miles west of Denton. Believing they were temporarily safe from pursuit, the outlaws were surprised by the arrival of a force of some forty men consisting of Texas Rangers and members of a local posse. During the ensuing shootout, Arkansas Johnson was killed. Henry Underwood was badly wounded but managed to climb onto his horse and escape. During the melee, Bass and three other outlaws snuck away. They hid in a nearby cave while the lawmen searched for them, sometimes coming so close that the bandits could hear their conversations. At some point during the night, Bass and his companions slipped away.

On July 18, Bass and three gang members, Frank Jackson, Seaborn Barnes, and Jim Murphy, rode into Round Rock, Texas, located about two hundred miles south of Denton. Constantly on the run and short of money, Bass had made plans to rob the bank at Round Rock. Unknown to Bass, however, gang member Jim Murphy had turned informant.

Murphy, who earlier had been arrested for train robbery, was awaiting trial when he was approached by authorities and offered a deal. If Murphy would agree to betray Bass, he would spare himself a long sentence in a federal prison. Murphy capitulated. It was agreed that the prosecutors would announce that Murphy had skipped bond when, in truth, he was released to rejoin Bass and the gang.

The gang members were suspicious of Murphy, calling him a traitor, and Seaborn Barnes urged Bass to kill him. Bass confronted Murphy. Murphy professed loyalty but Bass didn't believe him and had decided to kill him, when Frank Jackson stepped forward and vouched for Murphy's loyalty. Bass decided to spare him.

As Bass and the gang rode south, they stopped at Belton, where Bass sold a horse he had stolen days earlier in Waco. As this transaction was going on, Murphy seized the opportunity to steal away and send word to Texas Ranger major John B. Jones that Bass was on his way to Round Rock to rob the bank. Jones sent a small detachment of Rangers from Austin to Round Rock to await Bass and the gang, and then Jones made arrangements to join them.

Riding hard, the Rangers had arrived in Round Rock the previous day and made preparations for an ambush in the event that Bass showed up. More Rangers had been alerted and were on their way. They were neither expecting nor ready for an early appearance by the outlaw and his brigands.

After riding into Round Rock on tired mounts, Bass, Jackson, and Barnes went to one end of the town to a store owned by Henry Koeppel. Murphy rode to another store at the opposite end of town. If they found both ends of town relatively clear and free of lawmen, the outlaws planned to rendezvous at Koeppel's Store. From there, they intended to proceed on to the bank and rob it.

As Bass, Jackson, and Barnes approached Koeppel's Store, deputy sheriff Maurice Moore spotted them. It appeared to Deputy Moore that Bass carried a holstered revolver under his coat. Moore immediately alerted another nearby deputy, A. M. Grimes, who followed the gang members into the store.

Although Moore and Grimes had been advised that Sam Bass and his gang were likely to be in the area, the two lawmen did not recognize the outlaw; nor did they remotely suspect that the man might be dangerous. While Moore waited outside, Grimes approached Bass in the store, placed a hand over the bulge in his coat, and asked the newcomer if he was carrying a weapon. In response, Bass yanked the revolver from the holster and shot Grimes. As the startled deputy stumbled back toward the front door before collapsing, Moore drew his handgun and fired at Bass, striking the outlaw in the right hand and damaging the middle and ring fingers. A second later, the three train robbers fled the store, firing at deputy Moore as they ran. Moore was struck in the chest but continued shooting at the gang members.

At the first sound of the shooting at Koeppel's Store, the Texas Rangers gathered and raced to the scene. Spotting the fleeing Bass, Barnes, and Jackson, they opened fire. Ranger George Harrell took careful aim and shot Bass, the bullet striking him one inch to the left of his spinal column. Bass staggered and dropped to the ground. (Another account maintains that Texas Ranger Dick Ware fired the crippling shot.)

Seaborn Barnes, who had been running alongside Bass, was struck in the head and was likely dead before he hit the ground. Frank Jackson paused in his flight long enough to help Bass to his feet. Firing his revolver at the Rangers with one hand, he used the other to assist Bass onto his horse. As the Rangers closed in, the plucky Jackson stood his ground and kept up a steady fire. During a lull in the gun battle, Jackson mounted his own horse and, leading Bass's mount, rode away.

Putting his spurs to his horse, Jackson and the badly wounded Bass made their way out of Round Rock toward the north. They paused momentarily at a cemetery where they had earlier cached a rifle. After retrieving the weapon, Jackson remounted, and the two sped away once again. It was all Bass could do to stay in the saddle. He lost his grip and almost fell off his horse several times. Once out of sight of their pursuers, the two outlaws turned west into a dense oak wood.

Weakened by intense pain and loss of blood, Bass finally fell from his saddle. Jackson bandaged the leader's wounds as best he could, pulled him a short distance off the trail, and tried to make him comfortable. It was clear to Jackson that Bass's wounds were serious and that the outlaw did not have long to live. Bass encouraged his partner to leave him, to escape. At first Jackson refused, but Bass soon talked him into mounting his horse and riding away. Sam Bass was now left to fend for himself. Writhing in severe pain, he lay on the ground near Brush Creek all night long, too weak to continue his flight.

By dawn, Bass had lost a considerable amount of blood. Barely able to stand, he staggered away from his hiding place. After covering almost a half mile and in severe agony, he arrived at a house located not far from where a new spur of the International and Great Northern Railroad was being constructed. Several railroad workers engaged in laying track spotted Bass, barely alive, but continued with their work. They were too far away to discern that the man was badly wounded.

As he approached the house a woman exited the front door and spotted him. She immediately noticed his blood-soaked clothing. She called to her servant girl, and as the two started to run away, Bass called out to the woman, telling her he was desperately in need of a cup of water. Having difficulty speaking, he rasped out that he would go sit at the base of a nearby tree if she would send him one. The woman instructed the servant girl to deliver a cup of water to the newcomer, but by the time she brought Bass the cup, he was too weak to raise it to his lips.

A short time later a squad of Texas Rangers searching throughout the area arrived at the railroad construction site. They spotted Bass lying still and quiet beneath a live oak tree but mistook him for one of the railroad workers taking a nap. As the Rangers approached, Bass raised an arm and said, "Don't shoot. I'm Sam Bass." The Rangers transported the outlaw into Round Rock and placed him in the care of a physician, though it was clear he would not live long.

Texas Ranger major John B. Jones sat beside Bass in the doctor's office during most of his remaining time. Jones interrogated Bass about his gang members and tried to learn some information about where they might have gone into hiding. Bass was too weak to converse and fell asleep.

The next morning Jones once again took a seat next to the dying Bass and questioned him further. Bass provided a bit of information on the members of the gang who had been killed but none at all on the survivors. He told Jones he would not betray his friends. After several minutes of conversation, Bass fell silent for a while and then closed his eyes as if to sleep. A few moments later he opened them and looked around as if confused and frightened. He said, "The world is a-bobbin' around." Those were his last words. Sam Bass died the following day, July 21. It was his twenty-seventh birthday. He was buried in the Round Rock cemetery next to Seaborn Barnes.

Jim Murphy, whose betrayal of Sam Bass led to the outlaw's death, fled back to Denton. Word reached him that Frank Jackson was hunting him, intending to kill him for his treachery. Murphy turned himself in to the Denton sheriff and requested that he be placed in custody for protection. While staying at the jail, Murphy developed an eye infection. A physician gave him some medicine, cautioning him that it was for external use only. If ingested, it was toxic. Murphy committed suicide by drinking the entire contents of the vial.

Sam Bass was a pioneer of sorts. The intrepid outlaw introduced train robbery to the state of Texas, a type of banditry unheard of in the region until his arrival. With Bass's death, train robberies in Texas halted, but only for a time. Just as railroad and law enforcement officials were beginning to breathe a bit easier, convinced that such depredations might now be a thing of the past, renewed train robbery activity burst onto the Texas scene.

CHAPTER 7

THE BURROW GANG

If Sam Bass and his short-lived career of train robbery can be credited with introducing this form of banditry to Texas, then Rube Burrow was the obvious heir apparent. According to a number of researchers, Reuben "Rube" Burrow, along with his gang, was one of the most prolific train robbers in the history of the United States. Though not as well known as Jesse James, Butch Cassidy, Sam Bass, and others, Burrow (whose name is sometimes spelled Burrows) successfully robbed more trains than any of them. He has been credited with eight robberies, four in Texas and the others in Arkansas, Alabama, Louisiana, and Indian Territory (now Oklahoma). Active throughout much of the 1880s and 1890s, Burrow was known as the "King of the Train Robbers" and hunted by hundreds of lawmen and private detectives. He no doubt would have added to his total of train holdups were it not for his demise at the hands of the law.

Rube Burrow, along with his brother Jim, a prominent member of his gang, had his origins in Lamar County, northeastern Alabama. Rube was born Rueben Houston Burrow on December 11, 1854. Brother James Buchanan Burrow followed in 1858. In all, their parents had ten children. Their father, Allen Burrow, was a successful farmer who fought in the Civil War. He supplemented his farming income by producing a high-quality moonshine for which there grew a great demand. By Lamar County, Alabama, standards, the family prospered.

Rube Burrow

Reuben's mother, Martha Terry Burrow, was known throughout the area as an occultist and faith healer. Her clients referred
to her as Dame Burrow. People would arrive at the Burrow home
from miles around to have maladies treated by Mrs. Burrow's various incantations. Her more passionate followers claimed she could
cure arthritis, headaches, and even cancer. The more skeptical of
the area citizens referred to her as a witch.

As a youth, Reuben had a tendency to get into trouble.
When he was only ten years old, he shot and killed a neighbor
boy, a sometime companion. Brought into court, Reuben pleaded

Jim Burrow

self-defense and was acquitted. At fifteen years of age, Reuben donned a mask, broke into a neighbor's house, and stole several dollars. The youth was recognized and reported. On learning of this transgression, his father made him return the money.

For reasons not clear, Rube purchased a fake beard and a wig from a mail order house. When the package arrived at the post office in Jewell, Alabama, some of the hair was sticking out of one side of the box. Rube sent a friend to the post office to retrieve the package, but the postmaster, Moses J. Graves, refused to turn it over. On learning of this, an incensed Rube Burrow traveled to the post office, retrieved the package, and shot Graves through the heart. As there were no witnesses to the murder, Burrow was never arrested or charged.

Despite the family farm's success, Reuben Burrow decided early on that he was not cut out for what he regarded as the tedium and drudgery of planting, tending, and harvesting crops. Instead, he longed for adventure. He read books and articles describing the dynamic and exciting events related to the settling of the West, and, like Sam Bass, he was determined to travel there and see it for himself.

When he was eighteen, Rube Burrow left the Deep South and journeyed to Texas. Shortly after arriving in Stephenville in 1872, he made his way northeast to Wise County, where he found employment with his Uncle Joel on a farm. While farming still did not satisfy his lust for adventure, Burrow needed an income.

In addition to planting crops, Joel had a modest herd of cattle, and Burrow directed most of his attention to these animals. In time he became a competent cattleman and decided that he wanted to own his own farm and raise cattle.

The frugal Burrow saved his money and after a few years purchased a significant piece of property not far from Fort Worth. On this land he established a herd of cattle and devoted his time to becoming a successful cattleman. For a time he prospered, even earning a reputation as a skilled horseman. In 1876, Rube Burrow married Virginia Alverson and fathered two children. With his boyish good looks, a somewhat humble demeanor, strong work ethic, and attention to detail, Burrow appeared to be on his way to becoming a respectable citizen.

Then calamity struck the young family. A short time after giving birth to their second child, Virginia contracted yellow fever and died. The loss of his wife had a profound effect on Burrow. He was never the same after Virginia's death, and according to some observers, the event caused him to give up his farm and eventually led him down a path of lawlessness.

When he wasn't tending to the responsibilities of maintaining his ranch, Burrow found employment with the railroads, first with the Fort Worth and Denver line and later with the Texas and Pacific Railway. At least one writer has claimed that while working for the railroads, Burrow was gripped by the notion that robbing trains would be easy. A few researchers have suggested that Burrow was fascinated with the outlaw Jesse James and his perceived skills related to robbing trains. To Burrow, the daily grind of ranching could not compare with what he perceived as the glamour and thrill of stopping a train and stealing whatever money and valuables it carried.

In 1884, brother Jim arrived in Texas and joined Reuben. In that same year, Reuben remarried, this time to Adeline Hoover. By 1886, Burrow's ranch was proving unproductive, and he was unable to make a living. Shortly afterward, he and his second wife separated. Burrow, along with his brother Jim, went to work once again for Uncle Joel on another farm, this one in Erath County.

At age thirty-two, Burrow decided it was time to try his hand at outlawry. Having been inspired earlier in his life by the outlaw Jesse James, he was also impressed with what he discovered about the Texas train robbery activities of Sam Bass a few years earlier. The fact that Bass had been pursued by law enforcement authorities and subsequently killed did not seem to deter Burrow.

Researchers disagree about why Burrow took to robbing trains. Some have suggested that he found life on the farm tiresome and dull and barely earned enough money to pay bills and support his family. Burrow himself expressed his displeasure with such work. Others have suggested Burrow craved adventure and found an outlet for his yearning in train robbery. In the end, he found adventure and occasionally made off with significant money. Today, Burrow is regarded as one of Texas's most successful train robbers.

CHAPTER 8

BELLEVUE, TEXAS

December 1, 1886

During a return trip to his Texas farm from Oklahoma, Reuben Burrow, together with his brother Jim and two farmhands named Henderson Bromley (sometimes spelled Brumley) and Nep Thornton, decided to rob a train. Burrow and his companions had gone to Oklahoma, according to some researchers, on a farm-related trip to acquire livestock. Others insist the men traveled there to rob a wealthy widow.

Burrow decided to rob the Fort Worth and Denver (FW&D) passenger train while it was idling at the tiny community of Bellevue, located thirty miles southeast of Wichita Falls. At 11:00 a.m. on December 1, 1886, the FW&D stopped at a water tank three hundred yards west of the Bellevue depot.

Avoiding the crowd and several railroad employees milling about the depot, Burrow and his gang covered their faces with bandannas and approached the locomotive from the side opposite the station so they wouldn't be seen. Thornton climbed into the cab and held the engineer and fireman at gunpoint. Burrow led the other two gang members to the first passenger coach, which they boarded. With revolvers in hand, Burrow announced the holdup and ordered the passengers to turn over their watches, jewelry, and money.

It is believed that the conductor had alerted the passengers to the holdup only minutes earlier, giving them ample time to hide many of their valuables under the seats before the robbers arrived. After entering each of the coaches, the three outlaws moved slowly down the aisles while instructing the passengers to remove everything from their pockets and turn the items over to them. By the time the robbers had passed through the last of the cars, they had harvested less than $300, to them a disappointing amount.

In the last car, Burrow was surprised to encounter three armed soldiers who were escorting several prisoners to Fort Worth. Initially, a shootout was anticipated, but instead of resisting the robbers, the soldiers, concerned about the lives of the nearby passengers should shooting break out, allowed themselves to be disarmed. Burrow and his gang members relieved the soldiers of their weapons and stuffed them into their belts. The gang used at least two of the handguns in later train robberies.

Burrow offered to free the prisoners. At first the convicts considered it, but in the end refused. The soldiers were subsequently disciplined by their superiors for their inaction.

Since this was his first train robbery, the excitement of the undertaking, along with his inexperience, caused Burrow to completely forget about the express car, which was likely carrying several thousand dollars in cash. On the other hand, it might have been difficult to breach the express car since it was close to the station and near so many witnesses, many of whom were armed.

After riding away from the scene of the heist, Rube Burrow, though disappointed with this first effort, decided that robbing trains was where his talents lay. Burrow also figured the payoff from a successful heist would be greater than what resulted from the hard work he invested in raising cattle and maintaining a farm. Inspired by the possibilities, Burrow reviewed the mistakes made during the Bellevue robbery and began making plans for the next one.

CHAPTER 9

GORDON, TEXAS

January 23, 1887

Less than two months after his first successful train robbery, Rube Burrow, imbued with confidence and excited about the possibility of acquiring a lot of money, decided to try another. For his second attempt he set his sights on the small town of Gordon, in Palo Pinto County, about seventy miles west-southwest of downtown Fort Worth. Burrow learned that a Texas and Pacific train pulled into the station daily at 2:00 a.m., a time when few people were around to serve as witnesses or offer resistance.

Accompanied by Henderson Bromley, Burrow snuck aboard a passenger coach on the eastbound train while it was stopped at Gordon. A half hour later, the train departed the station and proceeded down the track. When the train was several miles out of Gordon, the two outlaws left the passenger car and, revolvers in hand, scrambled up and over the coal tender and into the cab of the locomotive. They placed the muzzles of their weapons against the necks of the startled engineer and fireman.

Burrow instructed the engineer to stop the train at a selected location another mile down the track. When the train pulled to a halt, brother Jim Burrow, along with Nep Thornton and a new gang member, Harrison Askew, stepped out of hiding and approached the idling engine. Askew, a hard-looking man with evil eyes, had arrived at Burrow's farm weeks earlier seeking work. He claimed to be an ex-convict. When he learned that Burrow was making plans to rob trains, Askew was eager to join the gang.

The engineer and fireman were ordered out of the cab at gunpoint and marched back to the express car. On arriving, Burrow hammered at the door with his fists and demanded that the messenger open up with all haste. At this moment, the train conductor stepped out onto the platform of one of the passenger cars to ascertain why the train had stopped. Spotting the engineer and fireman among the group of outlaws, he called out to them asking about the reasons for the delay. A response came in the form of a sudden volley of shots from Rube Burrow and Thornton.

From inside the express car, the messenger heard the shots and doused his lantern. Burrow hammered on the door and demanded that it be opened. His order was met with silence. He repeated his demand several times but received no response. Burrow then threatened to kill the engineer if the messenger did not cooperate. This threat was greeted with even more silence. Angered and growing frustrated with the delay, Burrow shot several holes in the door of the car. The response from the messenger was only more silence.

Burrow had already spent more time on the robbery than he intended. Tersely, he informed the messenger that if he did not open the door, the car would be set afire, and he would be burned alive. Apparently this threat carried more weight than that to kill the engineer. A few moments later, the messenger slid the door open and stepped aside, allowing Burrow and Bromley to clamber into the car. Forced to comply at gunpoint, the messenger opened the safe from which Burrow withdrew just under $3,000.

After pocketing the cash from the safe, Burrow and his men, along with the messenger, engineer, and fireman, proceeded toward the mail car. After gaining entrance with less difficulty than they had experienced with the express car, they removed $2,000 from a sack of registered mail.

At this point, Askew and Bromley were sent to retrieve the horses. After stuffing the money into saddlebags, the gang mounted up. Before riding away they fired their weapons into the air in an effort to discourage passengers and crew from exiting the coaches. Leaving the scene of the crime, the gang rode hard in a northerly direction for two hours, backtracked for several hundred yards, then turned toward the east and made their way across a stretch of rocky ground where they left no tracks.

Several hours after the robbery was reported, a posse arrived at the scene of the crime. The train had not moved from the site. After speaking with the engineer and fireman, the lawmen found the tracks of the outlaws nearby and followed them. A short time later, however, they lost the trail on the open prairie.

Rube Burrow was later identified as the leader of the train robbers, and before long wanted posters were tacked up throughout the region. Burrow decided it would be prudent to lay low for a while, but his mind reeled with the possibilities of future train robberies. In time, he set his sights on a Texas and Pacific Express that stopped at Benbrook, Texas, a small community near Fort Worth. While Burrow was making his plans, another gang struck at McNeill, Texas.

CHAPTER 10

McNEILL, TEXAS

May 18, 1887

While Rube Burrow was biding his time at his farm and making plans for his next train heist, a gang of a dozen mysterious outlaws pulled off the robbery of a Missouri Pacific express train at the small town of McNeill, thirteen miles north of Austin. The Missouri Pacific line was owned by railroad magnate Jay Gould. At one time, Gould was the leading railroad developer and speculator in America.

Around the time of the McNeill train robbery, Gould was generally recognized as the richest man in America. In addition to the Missouri Pacific, he owned the Union Pacific, the Texas and Pacific, the Wabash, and the St. Louis and Northern, a tenth of all railroad lines in the United States.

Despite his wealth, or perhaps because of it, Gould was also one of the most despised and reviled men in America. His efforts to corner the US gold market in 1869 had generated a stock market crash and created business panic nationwide. Gould's list of enemies was a long one, and some researchers believe the Missouri Pacific robbery at McNeill represented an effort by somebody, or somebodies, to get back at the entrepreneur.

A few minutes before 9:00 p.m. on May 18, 1887, ten to twelve masked, armed, and at the time unidentified men entered the McNeill train station. In addition to the railroad station, the town boasted a dozen houses and a general store. A nearby strip mine where lime was collected provided employment for most of the male residents. While one of the outlaws held the agent at gunpoint, others walked out onto the loading platform to await the train, and several more positioned themselves close to a nearby railroad switch. The Missouri Pacific connected Austin with Marble Falls and Burnet. The railroad was employed to haul large granite blocks from Marble Falls to Austin for the construction of the capitol building.

As the train slowed to a stop, a number of passengers rose from their seats and queued up at the door, preparing to disembark. At the same time, a porter climbed down from the locomotive and walked along the tracks toward a switch he had been instructed to throw, which would allow the train to continue east toward the town of Taylor, thirty miles away. Standing near the switch was what the porter later described as a "group of rough-looking men." As the porter approached, the strangers pulled revolvers from their holsters and began shooting at him. They fired over his head in an attempt to frighten him, which worked well since the porter turned and scurried back toward the train.

Before the doors to the passenger cars were opened, the armed men from the switch had rejoined their companions waiting on the platform. When the travelers spotted the gunmen they grew concerned. An instant later the outlaws fired into the coaches, forcing the passengers to take cover. Over one hundred shots were fired in only a few seconds. Windows were shattered, and the sides and ceilings of the coaches were riddled with bullet holes. One passenger, a salesman named Harry Landa, was slow to take cover and sustained a bullet wound to one arm.

The train robbers had no plans to relieve the passengers of their money. They merely wanted to keep them occupied during the heist so they would not interfere with the break-in to the express car. It has been reported that the express car was carrying $40,000. The man identified as the leader of the train robbers was described as tall and slender and wearing what appeared to be a fake beard.

With the passengers and crew cowering between the seats and on the floor, the gang moved on to the express car. When they received no response after knocking on the door, the outlaws forced it open. Inside they encountered two messengers who provided no resistance whatsoever. One of the robbers stepped forward, leveled a revolver at one of the messengers, a man named A. J. Nothacker, and ordered him to open the safe and hand over the money. The frightened Nothacker dutifully obeyed and passed the robber a small packet of bills. Angered, the outlaw cracked Nothacker across the head with the butt of his weapon.

When the remainder of the money had been removed from the safe, the robbers turned their attention to the mailbags at the other end of the express car. Robert Spaulding, the railroad mail clerk, was also on duty in the car. Spaulding decided to offer no resistance to the armed outlaws. He informed the robbers that the train was not transporting any registered mail, that it had all gone out on an earlier run. The robbers standing next to Spaulding told him that they were only after Jay Gould's money, not the government's.

When the train robbers were satisfied that they had accomplished all they had set out to do on this venture, they politely bade Spaulding a pleasant good evening, mounted their horses, and rode away. The amount of money taken was estimated by various officials to be between $21,000 and $55,000. Later investigations revealed that not all the money transported in the express car was taken, and it was assumed the robbers simply missed some of it among the packages, bundles, and sacks.

Law enforcement authorities were notified of the robbery as soon as possible. In Austin, a posse was formed and led by Travis County deputy sheriff Sam Platt and a Marshal Lacy (sometimes spelled Lucy). They were joined by a Sheriff Olive. The lawmen arrived at the scene of the robbery four hours later.

The posse picked up the tracks of the train robbers within minutes and tracked them to a location only half a mile from McNeill, where they had stopped to build a fire and cook a meal. Near the embers of the campfire, one of the posse members found a piece of paper that tied the robbers to a man named Joe Barber. Barber was well known to the lawmen and had been involved in criminal activities in the past. Barber's brother, Austin, was at the time in the Huntsville prison for horse theft. Another brother, John, had recently been arrested for the same crime. Later, he would be indicted for murdering a Williamson County deputy sheriff. For several days following the robbery, reports of sightings of the gang poured into law enforcement offices from area citizens.

After the passage of a few more days, lawmen arrested Joe Barber, James and Abner Ussery, and John and Charles Craft. The prisoners were brought before a judge, who heard testimony from dozens of witnesses. In the end, the case was dismissed, and the charged men were set free.

Neither Joe Barber, the Ussery brothers, or the Craft brothers ever attempted to rob a train again. The other members of the outlaw gang were never arrested or initially identified, and their whereabouts remained a mystery.

CHAPTER 11

BENBROOK, TEXAS

June 4, 1887

Nearly six months had passed since Rube Burrow and his gang had robbed their last train. Some, in particular the railroad companies, were just waiting for the other shoe to drop. When it finally did on June 4, 1887, few were surprised. This time, the target of Burrow and his gang was the Texas and Pacific Express. The place was Benbrook, then a small community a few miles southwest of Fort Worth. Today, Benbrook is a suburb of that great city.

According to author Richard Patterson, the Benbrook train robbery is significant in that it is believed to be the first in which a railroad trestle was employed by the outlaws in order to make their job easier.

On the evening of June 4, the T&P Express was preparing to leave the station at Benbrook. The passengers had all boarded and were seated, the express car messenger and mail car clerk had completed their duties, and the engineer had concluded the departure protocol. When the train was only seconds from pulling away from the station, Rube Burrow and Henderson Bromley, their faces blackened with charcoal, stepped out of hiding and approached. Pulling themselves up the ladder at the rear of the tender, they climbed to the top and made their way toward the front of the car. As the train was picking up speed, the two outlaws dropped down into the cab of the locomotive, guns drawn. Burrow ordered the engineer to proceed on down the track, cross a deep gorge, and then stop the train on the far side of the trestle. Burrow instructed the engineer to make certain the locomotive and tender were on solid ground while the rest of the train was perched on the bridge. With two somewhat successful train robberies under his belt, Burrow reasoned that any of the T&P crew or passengers inclined to disrupt the robbery would find that having to walk down the narrow and rather precarious trestle put them at a significant disadvantage.

After the train was stopped, Burrow ordered the engineer and fireman to climb down from the cab. At the same time, Jim Burrow, along with another gang member named Bill Brock, rode out of their hiding place in some nearby brush, leading two additional horses. Rube Burrow instructed the engineer and fireman to negotiate the trestle and accompany him back to the express car. Jim Burrow and Brock had by then positioned themselves near the rear of the car, revolvers at the ready in the event that someone exited the door of the trailing passenger coach.

As with previous train robberies executed by Burrow, the express messenger refused to open the locked door. Burrow, holding his revolver to the head of the engineer, directed him to return to the engine, retrieve a crowbar, and return. Within minutes, the engineer was standing once again beside Burrow, who ordered him to pry open the express car door. Once the door was forced open and the messenger saw the gun pointed at the engineer, he raised his hands and offered no resistance.

Burrow and Bromley climbed into the express car, forced open the safe, and removed just under $2,000. Moments later, the Burrow brothers, Bromley, and Brock were mounted up and riding away.

At the first opportunity, a posse was formed to go in pursuit of the train robbers. Unfortunately, a dense thunderstorm struck the region within an hour after the holdup, and the downpour obliterated any tracks left by the outlaws. Once again, Burrow and his gang had made an effective escape following a relatively easy robbery.

With his confidence at a renewed high, Burrow lost no time in planning his next train robbery. Three and a half months would pass before the gang undertook the heist. Burrow decided to return to Benbrook to rob the same train at the same trestle. Before he did, however, other enterprising train robbers made their mark.

CHAPTER 12

ENTER BILL WHITLEY AND BRACK CORNETT

While Rube Burrow and his gang bided their time relative to pulling off another train robbery, others, who perceived the possibilities of garnering riches in the same manner, made their presence known.

Bill Whitley was no stranger to crime and violence. Born William Henry Whitley on September 7, 1864, on a farm in Itawamba County, Mississippi, he was the youngest of several children brought into the world by parents William Taylor Whitley and Elizabeth Henry Whitley. (At least one document states that Whitley was born in the town of Smithville in Monroe County, Mississippi.)

Bill Whitley's older brothers served in the Confederate Army during the Civil War. Following the conflict, the area around Itawamba County in northeastern Mississippi was characterized as "wild" with rampant and "violent lawlessness." Raids and killings were not uncommon sights for the young Whitley.

In 1884, one of Whitley's brothers was shot and killed by a lawman. Seeking revenge, and perhaps an outlet for his own explosive nature, Whitley went on a rampage and in the end was responsible for the killing of eight men. Though his family members insisted stories of his activities were exaggerated, there is no denying the facts on record.

Though the chronology is unclear, it is known that Whitley migrated to Texas (some say it was in the company of his parents) and for a time lived in Lampasas, where he pursued his criminal and brutal ways. There, he also courted and married Cordelia Lucinda Cox. (At least one publication gives her name as Cornelia Cox.) The union created some problems for the Cox family when some members were arrested and charged with harboring a criminal.

Bill and Lucinda became the parents of two daughters: Minnie Margaret, born in November 1884, and Temperance Alice, born in March 1886. Despite the responsibilities related to supporting a growing family, Whitley continued to pursue his criminal activities. Law enforcement authorities were constantly on his trail and

Bill Whitley

even posted watchmen near his home. Believing that he needed to remove himself from the Lampasas area, Whitley decided to leave his wife and children in the care of her brother while he fled to England. A short time later, the brother moved the family to Coryell County, Texas.

When Whitley returned to Texas, he immediately fell in league with a man named Brack Cornett. Braxton Cornett was born May 22, 1841, in Clinton County, Missouri, and raised in Goliad County, Texas. (One account lists his birthplace as Goliad County.) Little is known of Cornett's life prior to his joining up with Bill Whitley to rob banks and trains. He often went by the alias "Captain Dick."

Brack Cornett

Together, Whitley and Cornett put together a gang and became successful bank and train robbers. Law enforcement authorities who pursued the outlaws alternately referred to them as the Bill Whitley Gang and the Brack Cornett Gang.

During the year 1887, Whitley and Cornett, along with a band of ten additional outlaws, conducted a series of bank robberies from which they netted several thousand dollars. On February 15, 1888, Whitley, Cornett, and another ten men entered a bank in Cisco, Texas, minutes before closing time and asked cashier C. C. Leveaux for some change. When Leveaux looked up, he was staring into the barrels of several drawn revolvers. By the time the gang walked out of the bank, they had stolen $9,000 in gold and silver along with some bank notes. Stories circulated that the loot was buried somewhere near Cisco, but none of it has ever been recovered.

Though Bill Whitley and Brack Cornett were successful bank robbers, their outlaw reputation rests largely on their train robberies.

CHAPTER 13

FLATONIA, TEXAS
June 18, 1887

Before Rube Burrow and his gang could return to Benbrook to rob another Texas and Pacific train, yet another band of outlaws took over a Southern Pacific (SP) train near Flatonia, about midway between Houston and San Antonio. These bandits made off with thousands of dollars from the express car, as well as a significant amount of loot taken from the passengers. It was believed at the time that some members of the gang had previous train robbery experience, likely having participated in the McNeill heist.

As the eastbound Southern Pacific slowly pulled away from the Flatonia station at 12:30 a.m. on June 18, 1887, two men, apparently emulating the style of Rube Burrow and his gang, climbed aboard the back of the coal tender, made their way across the top of the fuel supply, and dropped down into the locomotive cab. By this time, so common was this boarding technique by train robbers that it remains surprising that the railroad companies were unprepared for the tactic. It would have been a simple matter for the railroad company to station armed guards in the cab alongside the engineer and fireman, but no attempt had been made to do so.

At first, the engineer, B. A. Pickens, thought the newcomers were hobos, and he ordered them off the train. In response, the two strangers pulled revolvers and held them to the heads of Pickens and the fireman. They then ordered Pickens to keep the train moving ahead at a slow rate of speed until they told him otherwise. After traveling about a mile and a half, one of the robbers instructed the engineer to stop the train after crossing a trestle a short distance ahead, where a large fire could be seen burning next to the track. In the light of the fire, Pickens could see what he later testified were five additional armed men poised to approach the train. Later, others estimated that the total number of robbers in waiting numbered at least ten. Parked just beyond the group of men was a wagon pulled by two horses.

When the train first came to a stop, the robbers held a short conference. During this time, engineer Pickens managed to slip away and make his way to the first passenger coach. There, he alerted the travelers as to what was about to transpire, warning them to hide as many of their valuables as they could under the seats. Word quickly spread to the other passenger cars. Moments later, the robbers entered the first car and with swift efficiency walked through the passenger coaches relieving travelers of what money, watches, jewelry, and other items they had been unable to conceal.

One of the train robbers, who was clearly one of the gang leaders, was referred to by his companions as "Captain Dick." From the time he boarded the train until he rode away with his gang, he constantly sucked on a stick of hard candy.

Seated in one of the passenger cars was a man named Quintas, who was reportedly a high-ranking colonel in the Mexican army. On learning that the train was being robbed, Quintas told his manservant sitting next to him to prepare his revolver. He boasted out loud to all within earshot that he would kill anyone who tried to rob him. By the time the bandits reached Quintas, however, the officer had apparently lost his nerve and was easily disarmed. The outlaw called Captain Dick approached Quintas, told him he did not like Mexicans, and said, "I would just as soon kill you as eat my breakfast." Nervous, the colonel handed over his billfold containing $400.

When the robbers reached the sleeping car, they came upon a passenger who was frantically trying to hide his money under a mattress. He was pulled aside and beaten. A search of his hiding place yielded over $1,000. In another sleeping compartment, two salesmen were held up. When they hesitated after being ordered to turn over their valuables, they, too, were beaten. A female passenger who was likewise slow in turning over her purse was slapped.

When the outlaws had finished with the coaches, they approached the express car several dozen yards away. Inside, Wells Fargo express messenger Frank Folger, on realizing that a robbery was taking place, began stuffing sacks of cash into the stove in the hope that the robbers would never think to search there. After forcing their way into the car, however, the bandits spotted Folger in the act of trying to hide the money. Angered, one of them cracked the messenger alongside the head with the butt of his revolver.

When the money bags had been retrieved from the stove, the robbers turned their attention to the safe, which could be opened only with a key. One of the bandits commented that moments before arriving at the express car he had seen the messenger toss what appeared to be a key out the express car door and that it had landed on the ground a short distance away. Folger was ordered to step outside the car and locate the key. When he refused, one of the bandits yanked a skinning knife from a belt scabbard and cut slits in both of his ears, with a promise of worse to come if he did not retrieve the key. With his hands held to his ears, the bleeding Folger set about trying to locate the key with no further resistance. After a few moments he found it and handed it over to one of the gang members.

With the same efficiency manifested from the beginning of the robbery, the outlaws opened the safe, removed the contents, jumped from the car, and ran toward their horses. Moments later they were riding away in different directions, firing their revolvers as they fled.

The total amount of loot taken during the robbery remains unclear. One account states that $600 was removed from the express car and another $1,000 from the passengers. Another report estimated the haul at more than $3,000.

In a short time, several posses were organized to pursue the train robbers, but success was slow in coming. A man named George Shoaf, a well-known gambler from San Antonio, was arrested and charged with participation in the robbery. Shoaf, however, vehemently denied any role in the event and said he could prove he was miles away from the robbery by calling on witnesses who had seen him playing poker in San Antonio. His alibi proved legitimate.

The robbery of the Southern Pacific train at Flatonia marked a significant change in method by the perpetrators. For the first time, passengers and crew were subjected to harsh and brutal—and by all accounts unnecessary—treatment by the bandits. Heretofore, passengers and crew were generally left unharmed unless they offered a threat. When news of the event made its way to the papers, the public reacted with anger and demanded that law enforcement authorities move quickly to arrest the gang. Texas governor Lawrence S. Ross likewise voiced outrage at the behavior of the train robbers and vowed to have them captured. Likely bending to the will of the powerful railroads, Ross announced that from that day on "five to ten well-armed fighting men" would be assigned to each train moving through the state of Texas. In order to accomplish this, Ross commissioned 390 new Texas Rangers.

Newspapers reported that Wells Fargo, the company that had charge of the express car that was robbed, offered a $1,000 reward for the "capture and conviction" of each of the robbers. Following this announcement, Governor Ross lost no time in adding $500 to that amount, along with a promise that the robbers would be caught. In addition, the Southern Pacific Company contributed

$250, and the US government kicked in another $200. In all, a total amount of $1,950 for the capture and conviction of each of the robbers was being dangled in front of the public in the hope that one or more citizens might come forth with information. It was not long in coming.

After reading an article about the Flatonia train robbery, a Giddings, Texas, resident named Mike Buck revealed that the leader of the gang was his "great-great grandfather" Bill Whitley. Though it seemed unlikely that such a generational gap could occur, especially since Whitley was only twenty-three years old, it was determined that Buck and Whitley were, in fact, close relatives. Buck said it was Whitley and another man named Brack Cornett who had boarded the train at Flatonia and forced the engineer to pull it to a stop. Buck also related that Whitley had been involved in the McNeill train robbery one month earlier. Whitley, known throughout this area of Texas as an unsavory character, had also robbed the First National Bank at Cisco, Texas.

The search for the Flatonia train robbers involved law enforcement authorities from the state of Texas, sheriff departments from the surrounding counties, Wells Fargo detectives, and local police officers, as well as citizens. The state of Texas, along with the US government, placed significant pressure on lawmen to bring the bandits to justice and provided a contingent of US marshals to assist in the pursuit.

Weeks passed, but lawmen remained hard on the trail of the train robbers. In September two men—Tom Jones and Jim Henson—were found and arrested in San Saba County for "illicit dealings in horse flesh." While in custody, Jones bragged to another prisoner about his role in the Flatonia train robbery. Not long afterward his jailers determined that Jones had indeed been part of the gang of bandits. Henson, as it turned out, was involved not only with the Flatonia train robbery but also with the one that occurred at McNeill.

Henson, who had earlier turned state's evidence related to a number of stagecoach robberies, was charged with complicity in the Flatonia robbery by San Saba sheriff Metcalf. Henson agreed to reveal the names of the gang members as well as provide evidence to convict them on the condition that he be released. A judge would not agree to such a stipulation but did promise a lighter sentence in return for his cooperation. With information provided by Henson, another of the gang members—John Criswell—was arrested several days later. More arrests followed.

At 10:00 a.m. on September 27, a number of the train robbers, shackled and chained, were arraigned before US commissioner Ruggles and US district attorney Kelborg. Though newspaper reports differ on the names of the robbers who appeared in court, it is likely that the list included Tom Jones, Jim Henson, John Criswell, Ed Reaves (alias Pat Reaves), J. A. "Bud" Powell (alias Charles Thompson), and a man named Humphries. The robbers remaining at large included Whitley, Brack Cornett (alias Captain Dick), John Hill, and John Barbour.

In the courtroom, the gang member identified as Humphries, hoping to escape a prison sentence, explained in detail how the entire Flatonia train robbery was planned and executed. He claimed he had no part in the robbery other than driving a wagon and was not involved with taking anyone's money. During his testimony, Humphries referred to the Flatonia train robbers as the Bill Whitley Gang. Of the men appearing in court, only J. A. Powell and Ed Reaves were made to stand trial. They were found guilty and sent to prison.

The remaining members of the gang who were still on the run—Whitley, Cornett, Hill, and Barbour—evaded capture and went on to attempt another train robbery, this one at Harwood, Texas (see chapter 15).

Despite Governor Ross's bombastic declarations and promises, train robberies in Texas did not decrease at all but in fact increased. As if the depredations of the Bill Whitley/Brack Cornett train robbers were not enough to be concerned with, in a very short time Rube Burrow and his gang were back in business. Remarkably, Burrow decided to return to Benbrook, the site of an earlier robbery, to make another attempt at pulling a heist on the same Texas and Pacific train.

CHAPTER 14

BENBROOK, TEXAS
September 30, 1887

Benbrook is the only location in the history of the state of Texas where the same train was robbed in the same location by the same gang of robbers. Only three and a half months had passed between the two heists.

Not only that, the same engineer and fireman were on duty during both robberies. Despite the uniqueness of this heist, details are sketchy, and newspaper reports of the time carried scant information about the event. Furthermore, the newspapers did little in the way of follow-up investigation and reporting. In the end, all that was known for certain was that the Rube Burrow Gang had struck again.

Repeating the procedure established during the first robbery, Rube Burrow and gang member Henderson Bromley scrambled aboard the Texas and Pacific train only a few minutes before it departed the station on September 30, 1887. As before, the two outlaws made their way across the coal tender and arrived at the locomotive cab where they instructed the engineer to stop the train. Recognizing the two robbers, the engineer and fireman seemed to know exactly what they needed to do. They offered no resistance and cooperated as best they could without saying a word.

Despite the earlier promises delivered by Texas governor Lawrence S. Ross relative to instituting protective measures for the railroads that operated in the Lone Star State, there were no guards, armed or otherwise, on duty on this particular T&P run. With little difficulty and encountering no resistance whatsoever, Burrow forced the express car door open, climbed in, and, holding the express messenger at gunpoint, removed just over $2,700 from the safe. Moments later, the outlaws rode away.

Coincidentally, as with the previous Benbrook train robbery by the Burrow Gang, a sudden and violent thunderstorm struck the region and washed away any tracks that might have been left. As a result, the subsequent posses were unable to determine the escape route of the outlaws. Lawmen ranged out in a variety of directions from the robbery site but had no luck picking up any sign of the bandits.

The second Benbrook train robbery marked the end of Rube Burrow's Texas outlaw career. Some researchers believe that he had plans to rob other trains in Texas but, shortly after the September 30 holdup, felt the pressure of lawmen closing in and decided to lay low for a time. Burrow chose to leave Texas. He fled to his home state of Alabama where he was taken in by relatives. Following more robberies in that state and others, Burrow finally met his end in a shootout with lawmen in 1890.

CHAPTER 15

HARWOOD, TEXAS
September 22, 1888

For the previous ten years, train robbery momentum had been building in Texas, slowly but most certainly. In the cases of Sam Bass and Reuben Burrow, multiple robberies were planned and executed by the same persons and their partners over and over. The Bill Whitley Gang, which had been involved in the train robberies at Flatonia and McNeill, had experienced some successes, but after the second heist half of the gang had been arrested, and a few had been tried, convicted, and sent to prison, with Whitley and Cornett still at large.

Though an experienced and successful train robber, as well as a bona fide bad man, Whitley never received the recognition or notoriety of a Sam Bass or a Reuben Burrow, although he was just as active and efficient. Though he was still on the run from the law for his involvement with the Flatonia and McNeill robberies, the bold and daring Whitley decided to undertake yet another. This one was to prove his undoing.

Whitley decided to rob the Southern Pacific train at Harwood, Texas, on September 22, 1888. Harwood was a small town located in Gonzalez County. For the job, Whitley relied on assistance from Braxton "Brack" Cornett. (Some researchers believe it was Cornett's idea to rob the train and that he enlisted Whitley to assist him.)

Somehow, rumor of a potential robbery of the SP train began to spread, and word eventually reached US marshal John Rankin. Assuming his information was accurate, Rankin decided to thwart the bandits by hiding in the train and surprising them when they arrived. Rankin recruited Deputy Duval West along with a number of Texas Rangers. They armed themselves, packed extra ammunition, and boarded the train on the appointed day and seated themselves in a passenger car.

After the last passenger was loaded and the express and mail cars secured, the train pulled away from the station with a loud whistle and a belch of black smoke from the locomotive. After traveling about three miles and picking up speed, the train was stopped by a gang of three robbers. Bill Whitley and Brack Cornett, along with a third outlaw whose identity is unknown, approached the passenger car. As they neared the coach, the lawmen opened fire, scattering the outlaws and ultimately driving them away.

In addition to thwarting the train robbery, the aggressive tactic employed by the lawmen was sufficient to send Whitley and Cornett into escape mode. Certain that a posse would not be long in tracking them, the three outlaws rode away from the robbery site as fast as possible. This time luck was not with them, for the determined lawmen pursued with the intent of not giving up until they had captured or killed the train robbers.

CHAPTER 16

THE KILLING OF BILL WHITLEY AND BRACK CORNETT

Following the botched robbery attempt on the Southern Pacific train at Harwood, a posse was not long in forming. From the site of the robbery, the posse immediately went in pursuit of the would-be robbers. For three days, the lawmen, composed primarily of US marshals, followed the tracks of the outlaws and finally caught up with and encountered them in Floresville, thirty-five miles southeast of San Antonio. While details are sketchy, it is known that when the marshals came upon the train robbers, a shootout took place. Whitley was killed at the onset of the skirmish, and the unidentified gang member was arrested. Seeing an opportunity to evade the lawmen, Cornett escaped on horseback.

Whitley was buried in the Mahomet Cemetery in Burnet County, Texas. According to extant documents, he was only twenty-four years old. His headstone reads, "He was a kind and affectionate husband, a fond father, and a friend to all." Undoubtedly, some of Whitley's victims would disagree with that epitaph.

Texas lawmen took up the chase after Cornett. There are three widely differing versions of how Cornett met his end. One version has him being overtaken by the pursuing posse and, following a brief gun battle, shot dead.

A second, more likely version has Cornett arriving at the ranch of a friend in La Salle County in southern Texas. The friend,

65

Alfred Allee, had learned of the recent attempt on the Southern Pacific train at Harwood and was aware that Cornett was involved. He was also aware that Cornett had participated in earlier train robberies. Allee, who was also alleged to be a Texas Ranger, regarded Cornett as dangerous and untrustworthy.

As Cornett rode up to the ranch house early one morning, Allee, who was eating breakfast, looked out the window and spotted him. After strapping on his gun belt and checking the loads in his revolver, the rancher went outside to meet him. As Cornett dismounted from his horse, Allee calmly walked up and shot him, killing him instantly.

A third version has Allee, in the capacity of a Texas Ranger, pursuing Cornett across three states to a location identified as Frio, Arizona. After Allee caught up with the train robber, a brief shootout occurred, with Cornett being killed.

That rancher/Ranger Allee received $3,800 in reward money for the killing of Brack Cornett provides evidence of the accuracy of one of the two latter versions.

With the deaths of Bill Whitley and Brack Cornett, the train-robbery gang the two men had formed was now leaderless. The few remaining members who were not in jail, on learning of the demise of their fellows, separated, went their own ways, and were never heard from again.

CHAPTER 17

THE DEMISE OF RUBE BURROW

After his second Benbrook train robbery, Rube Burrow became an oft-hunted man. Wanted posters had been tacked up throughout much of the Lone Star State and his identity made known to railroad detectives, sheriff departments, local police, and other law enforcement agencies. Gathering his loot and his gang, Burrow decided it was time to leave the area for a while. He made plans to travel back to his childhood home in Lamar County, Alabama, far enough from Texas that he was certain he would not be hounded by pursuit.

On arriving in Alabama, Burrow presented his relatives with gifts, all purchased with the money stolen during his Texas train robberies. The brothers, Reuben and Jim, along with Bill Brock, were welcomed and assured by family members that they could hide out for as long as necessary in this sparsely populated northwestern Alabama county.

After arriving in Alabama, the Burrow Gang, wishing to impress relatives, lived lavishly, and it wasn't long before their money ran out. The easiest way to get more, reasoned Rube, was to do what he felt he did best: rob another train. After considering a number of options, the outlaws set their sights on a St. Louis, Arkansas, and Texas Railway train two states away at Genoa, Arkansas. The robbery took place on December 9, 1887. Unlike in their previous robberies, the Burrow Gang got careless on this outing. Unfortunately for the three bandits, they left their raincoats at the scene. Markings inside the slickers led to their identification, and within weeks dogged Pinkerton detectives traced the Burrow Gang to their Lamar County hideout.

As the Pinkertons were closing in, informants alerted the Burrow Gang to their proximity. Prior to storming the Burrow hideout, the detectives hung wanted posters for the outlaws throughout that part of the South. Eluding the Pinkertons only scant hours before they arrived, the train robbers escaped on foot. A few days later, they purchased passage on a Louisiana and Nashville (L&N) train and traveled to Montgomery, Alabama, where they intended to go into hiding until things cooled down.

The L&N train made several stops along the route. As it made its way toward Montgomery, a sharp-eyed train conductor recognized the Burrow Gang from the wanted posters. At the next stop, the conductor left the train, went to the telegraph office, and alerted officials at the Montgomery station. When the train arrived, a squad of policemen was waiting to apprehend the Burrow Gang.

On their arrest, Rube Burrow argued with the officers that they were victims of a case of mistaken identity. He insisted that he, Jim, and Brock were representatives of a timber company and had arrived in town to conduct business. The lawmen did not fall for the explanation and decided to transport the three men to the police station, where they intended to interrogate them further. Though the three passengers were initially identified as members of the notorious Burrow Gang, the policemen, in a lapse of good judgment, did not search any of them for weapons. Each of the gang members was carrying a revolver under his coat.

As the three robbers were being shepherded into the police station, Rube Burrow saw a chance for escape and took it. When the policeman escorting him looked away for a moment, Rube turned and made a break for freedom. The officer reached for his revolver, but in the process his coat got caught on a doorknob, distracting him momentarily. By the time the policeman got his weapon out, Rube was long gone.

Jim Burrow was less fortunate. As he attempted to flee, he was immediately tackled and wrestled to the ground, where he was cuffed. Thirty minutes later he was locked in a jail cell. Jim was subsequently sent to Arkansas to stand trial for the Genoa robbery.

As Rube Burrow was running away from the police station, he glanced back and spotted a man pursuing him. Believing the pursuer to be a policeman, Burrow pulled his revolver from beneath his coat, turned, aimed, and fired two shots, each of them striking the man. The chaser stumbled, then fell to the ground, severely wounded and writhing in pain. As it turned out, the victim was not a policeman at all, but a newspaper reporter who was after a story. It took him several weeks to recover.

Rube Burrow fled down alleys and between houses and managed to elude his trackers. He reached the outskirts of town with little difficulty. Spotting the edge of a thick wood one hundred yards beyond, he fled in that direction. Hardened by years of heavy work on his farm and quite at home in the Alabama woods, Burrow had no trouble distancing himself from the lawmen bent on his recapture. He knew how to survive and move about in this kind of environment and was far more comfortable in such surroundings than those who were tracking him.

While reports of Rube Burrow sightings arrived at police stations from time to time, and while trackers often came upon recently vacated campsites believed to have been occupied by him, the train robber always managed to evade his pursuers. In all, the wily Burrow succeeded in dodging the law in this manner for two years.

Burrow eventually made it back to the friendly environs of Lamar County and his family. Lawmen, however, had been watching the location and soon learned their quarry was in the region. They began closing in again, making it difficult for Rube to stick around. Realizing it was just a matter of time before he was apprehended once again, Burrow snuck away from Lamar County. This time he fled to Florida, where he believed he would be safe. There, he worked for a time in the turpentine camps.

While spending time in relative safety in the Sunshine State, Burrow fell in with a man named Leonard Brock (no relation to gang member Bill Brock). Together, the two made plans to travel to Arkansas to spring brother Jim from jail. Their plans never materialized. Only a few days before they were ready to take action, Burrow and Brock learned that Jim had become ill and died while incarcerated.

Rube Burrow had run out of money. Again, he decided the best and easiest way to obtain more was to resort to what he believed was his only option: train robbery. While he and Leonard Brock were on the run, Rube went on a train-robbing spree that lasted nearly two years. On December 15, 1888, Burrow and Brock robbed the Illinois Central train at Duck Hill, Mississippi, taking a significant amount of money from the express car.

On September 25, 1889, Burrow, Brock, and a new gang member named Rube Smith (also Burrow's cousin) stopped the Mobile and Ohio train on a trestle near Buckatunna, Mississippi. In all, they took $5,000 from the mail and express cars but somehow overlooked $70,000 in brand-new currency packed in boxes next to the express car door.

Rube Burrow undertook his next, and final, train robbery as a solo act. It has never been clear why his gang members were not involved, but on the evening of September 1, 1890, Burrow stopped an L&N train over a trestle spanning the Escambia River in northwestern Florida. After taking money from the express car,

Burrow fled, but law enforcement authorities immediately picked up his trail.

Louisville and Nashville railroad detectives collaborated with investigators associated with the Southern Express Company to put an end to Burrow's train-robbing depredations once and for all. Nearly a month following his robbery of the L&N train, Burrow was tracked to the tiny farm community of Repton, Alabama, northeast of Mobile. The manhunt continued for another full year, sometimes with the detectives closing in, other times with Burrow eluding pursuit and vanishing for weeks at a time. On occasion, Burrow abandoned a hiding place only minutes before detectives arrived.

Finally, on October 7, 1890, Burrow was tracked to a cabin a short distance west of Myrtlesville, Alabama. Lawmen closed in, and with the place surrounded by more than twenty armed law enforcement personnel, Burrow surrendered. He was placed in irons and transported to the nearby county seat at Linden. On arriving, Burrow's captors found the jail locked and the sheriff unavailable. They marched the outlaw to an unoccupied office next door and locked his chains to an iron ring fastened to the floor. Two deputies, John McDuffie and Jesse Hildreth, along with another man, stood guard. Deputy J. D. Carter and a fifth deputy were sleeping in an adjacent building.

During the night, Burrow, who had not eaten for nearly twenty-four hours, complained of hunger and requested that one of the deputies bring him a cloth sack that had been in his possession at the time of capture. The sack, Burrow explained, had some food in it. Deputy McDuffie made a casual inspection of the sack and saw that it contained some ginger snaps. He handed it over to Burrow. A moment later, Burrow pulled a revolver from the sack and pointed it at the surprised, and careless, McDuffie, who had not only failed to detect the heavy revolver in the sack but left his own handgun lying on a table several feet away. Inexplicably, the two other deputies, who by now had awakened, were unarmed.

At gunpoint, Burrow ordered Deputy Hildreth to lead him to Deputy Carter. During the capture of Burrow, Carter had seized the train robber's rifle, and Burrow wanted it back. On arriving at the building where Carter and the other deputy were sleeping, Burrow instructed Hildreth to call out that a problem at the jail required his presence. Burrow then took up a position behind a nearby tree, his revolver at the ready.

When the sleepy Carter walked out the door strapping on his gun belt, Burrow called out to him and told him he wanted his rifle returned to him. Carter's response was to reach for his revolver. He was not fast enough. Before he could aim his weapon, Burrow shot him in the left shoulder. Undeterred, the plucky Carter got off four rapid shots. The last one struck Burrow. In an odd reaction, the outlaw leaped high into the air and then fell to the ground, where he writhed in pain. As witnesses gathered around the wounded man, they observed Burrow was gasping for air. A moment later, he was dead.

On October 9, the train transporting Rube Burrow's body pulled into the Sulligent station in Lamar County. Burrow's family members, who had been informed of his death and alerted to the arrival of the body, had gathered. The corpse of the now famous train robber had been placed in an inexpensive wooden casket. When the train finally came to a stop, the door to the express car slid open. In a deliberate show of contempt for the slain outlaw, a team of Southern Express Company officials who had been placed in charge of the body unceremoniously shoved the casket out of the car, causing it to land heavily on the station platform. Without a word, the express personnel slammed the car door closed. Moments later, the train, amid a blowing whistle and belching smoke, pulled away from the station.

A train, the object of so many of Rube Burrow's outlaw escapades, had delivered the now famous robber to the region of his final resting place.

With the end of Rube Burrow and the apparent dispersal of what little was left of his gang, railroad officials, particularly those in Texas, experienced relief. Finally, the scourge of rail companies was dead and would no longer menace express car shipments.

Their relief, however, was short-lived. Rather than ending, the problems with train robbers were about to begin anew. Outlaws like Sam Bass and Rube Burrow showed like-minded desperadoes how to accomplish a successful heist, and several enterprising train robbers seized the opportunity.

CHAPTER 18

BANGS, TEXAS

December 20, 1889

An unusual and somewhat unorthodox attempt at robbing a train occurred in the tiny community of Bangs on December 20, 1889. For the bandits, the adventure proved unsuccessful. Given the amount of money taken, the effort invested in the robbery was hardly worth it.

On December 22, 1889, a passenger train traveling west on the Pan-Angelo branch of the Santa Fe Railroad pulled into the station at Bangs, seventy miles southeast of Abilene. It had earlier departed Temple and was bound for Brownwood. As the train was idling, railway station guard Al Ward was standing next to the tracks near the engine, when four men approached him. Believing the men were simply on their way to the station, Ward was caught by surprise when the newcomers donned masks and drew their revolvers. They instructed the alarmed and frightened Ward to raise his hands and do what he was told if he didn't want to get hurt.

At that same moment, the brakeman, a man named Penn, arrived on the scene, discerned what was happening, and, as he was standing next to Ward, pulled the guard's revolver from his holster. Without saying a word, Penn fired into the midst of the gang, hitting no one. When the four startled outlaws regained their composure, they fired back at Penn. The brakeman was shot "through the bowels," a wound that proved fatal within a few hours.

As Penn lay writhing on the ground, the four men ordered Ward to uncouple the express car from the following coach. This done, they climbed into the cab of the locomotive and instructed the engineer to pull ahead several hundred yards and stop. Once the train halted, the robbers descended to the ground and walked back to the express car. One of the bandits hammered at its door with the butt of his revolver and demanded the messenger open up immediately. The messenger, a man named Dean, refused to comply.

Moments later, the engineer arrived and advised Dean to open the door before somebody got hurt. Dean slid the door open, and holding their handguns on the frightened messenger, the outlaws entered the express car. Unable to force open the safe, they called Dean over and instructed him to do it or suffer the consequences. The nervous messenger fumbled with the lock several times, failing to gain access. Frustrated, one of the outlaws cracked Dean across the head several times and ordered him to hurry up. The robbers took all the money they found in the safe, a total of only $42. After pocketing the bills, they jumped from the express car and ran from the scene, presumably to a location where they had picketed their horses.

Messenger Dean described the leader of the gang as standing five feet, seven inches tall and wearing dark pants with a dark overcoat. Two other gang members were dressed identically. The fourth man, according to Dean, remained a significant distance away while the robbery was taking place.

After the robbers made their escape, a posse was formed and, accompanied by bloodhounds, attempted pursuit. No one was ever apprehended, and the robbers' identities were never determined.

CHAPTER 19

TEMPLE, TEXAS
May 13, 1892

One of the most bizarre approaches to a train robbery ever to have occurred in history took place near Temple on May 13, 1892. Up to this time, a number of methods had been employed to stop trains around the country, almost all of them effective. They included piling obstacles such as rocks or trees across the tracks, starting a bonfire in the middle of the tracks, or simply standing on the track waving a red lantern, a signal to the engineer that danger lay ahead and the train should come to a stop. In many cases robbers, armed with handguns, traversed the coal tender, dropped into the cab of the locomotive, held a gun to the head of the engineer, and simply ordered him to halt the train.

On this night, a team of seven train robbers convinced two of their members to lie down on the track, each of them curled into a fetal position. As the regular run of a southbound Missouri, Kansas and Texas passenger train that was using the International and Great Northern tracks on that particular day approached the men on the tracks, the engineer spotted them in the headlight with plenty of time to apply the brakes. The engineer remained cautious, however, as this was a rather unusual occurrence. Though he slowed the train considerably before reaching the prone figures, the suspicious engineer kept it in motion, all the time scanning the surrounding area for any sign of bandits.

When the train was within ten feet of the men on the tracks, the two jumped up and fled. At that exact moment, the engineer throttled the train forward, full steam ahead. He was determined to thwart what he perceived to be a highly unorthodox robbery attempt.

As the train picked up speed, before it had covered much distance, the remainder of the gang dashed out of hiding. They were carrying rifles and shotguns and raced toward the passenger cars, their initial intent apparently being to board and rob those inside. While only a few yards from the cars, the outlaws stopped and began shooting, peppering the passenger cars, the express car, and the mail car with dozens of bullets and buckshot as the train gathered speed. Windows were shattered, and several passengers were injured, mostly from the broken glass. A conductor who was taking a nap in one of the sleeping cars was hit in the arm by a stray bullet.

The engineer never stopped the train, just held the throttle wide open to flee the scene as rapidly as possible. In only a few moments, the entire train had sped by the frustrated and dumbfounded robbers, leaving them standing helplessly beside the tracks.

When the train pulled in at the next station down the line, the robbery attempt was reported. A somewhat casual investigation was initiated, but no pertinent evidence of any kind was found. The identities of the would-be robbers were never determined, no arrests were made, and the robbery attempt was listed as unsolved.

CHAPTER 20

BRACKENRIDGE, TEXAS
June 25, 1893

Most of the train robberies in Texas up to this point had followed a pattern that deviated little from the earliest attempts. With minor exceptions, passengers and crew put up little to no resistance, remaining somewhat passive during the execution of the robbery. The exceptions were generally confined to various levels of defiance manifested by the express messengers. Their resistance likely stemmed from the notion that they were responsible for the contents of the car and stood to lose their jobs should something happen to the shipment.

The few who did put up some form of resistance were sometimes beaten and injured and rarely shot and killed. The train holdup near Brackenridge, Texas, on a warm June afternoon in 1893 represented a significant departure from the norm. In this case, both passengers and crew united to thwart the efforts of the would-be bandits, prevented a robbery, and brought one of the bandits to justice.

On this day, a San Antonio and Aransas Pass (SA&AP) train had departed Brackenridge and slowed for a curve just south of the small town in Wilson County, not far from San Antonio. The next scheduled stop was at Kenedy. Brackenridge was the largest train depot between San Antonio and Corpus Christi. The express car on this particular SA&AP run reportedly carried $50,000 in the safe.

A short distance ahead was the Indian River Bridge, a narrow trestle spanning the San Antonio River. Just prior to departing Brackenridge, the train had been approached by three men who slipped onto the platform of the baggage car. As the train pulled away from the station, one of the robbers, who later identified himself as John D. May, made his way to the top of the coal tender and perched there. He waited for the train to gain some distance from the town.

After about a mile, the man atop the coal tender shouted to the engineer, Mike Tierney, and the fireman, F. F. Martin, in the locomotive cab to raise their hands. When the railroad employees turned toward the source of the threat, they saw a man pointing two revolvers at them. Following a moment of stunned surprise, fireman Martin made a sudden move toward a box under the cab's seat and was immediately shot, struck by two bullets. One report has Martin dying from the gunshot wounds. Another report stated that the fireman fell from the engine, landed under the wheels of the train, and died a few minutes later.

Engineer Tierney began pulling the train to a stop. But May ordered him to proceed toward the Indian River Bridge before halting. According to one report, as the train was slowing, Tierney jumped out of the locomotive cab and searched for cover. The bandit who shot Martin then leaped from the tender into the locomotive cab and applied the brakes, eventually stopping the train.

A second version of the event has engineer Tierney, after being ordered to continue toward the bridge, moving his hands across the array of levers and controls as if complying with the order. Instead of advancing the throttle, however, he set the air brakes and locked them into position.

Frustrated, May attempted to get the train moving again and manipulate the throttle. Unable to make progress and overwhelmed with the task before him, he simply gave up and jumped from the cab to the ground. Frantic, he then ran toward the Indian River Bridge and the San Antonio River between the two rails.

When the two robbers who were still stationed on the platform of the baggage car saw the fireman fall to the tracks, they panicked. Killing had apparently not been part of their plan, and it unnerved them. They jumped from the train and fled toward the shelter of the nearby woods. As the robbers neared the trees, the train came to a stop.

By this time, the passengers and the rest of the train crew began to suspect something was amiss, and they soon determined that a robbery attempt was in progress. As it turned out, a large percentage of the passengers were armed men, most of them carrying revolvers. When they discerned what was taking place and saw the fleeing men carrying weapons and racing for the woods, they gave chase.

The conductor, Ed Steele, happened to arrive at the locomotive about the same time May jumped from the cab. Realizing what was happening, Steele hurried back to the end of the tender and uncoupled it from the rest of the train. Engineer Tierney, who had been watching the developments from hiding, climbed back into the engine cab, released the brakes, opened the throttle, and set off in pursuit of May. Just before the front car pulled away, conductor Steele and one of the passengers, George Butler, both men carrying revolvers, chased after the two bandits who were running toward the woods.

With engineer Tierney coaxing the locomotive to higher speed, it began gaining on May, who was curiously still running down the railroad bed in front of it. As Tierney closed the distance on May, he spotted three men who appeared to be waiting at the Indian River Bridge for the arrival of May and/or the train.

As unlikely as it seems, May continued to race down the tracks directly in front of the oncoming locomotive. In moments, the train was within only a few feet of the fleeing May, who looked back, saw the engine almost upon him, and at the last moment dashed off the tracks and ran toward the adjacent woods. Seeing this, his three companions, who were watching this odd chase from the bridge, likewise took flight and fell in close behind May.

As he spotted May and his three companions fleeing toward the woods, conductor Steele abandoned pursuit of the two robbers and turned his attention toward May and the others. May fired his weapon at his pursuers as he went. His lead over his three cohorts increased, and he disappeared into a dense cluster of trees. The three men from the bridge paused long enough to turn and fire back at the pursuing conductor, but none of their bullets found their mark. By this time, engineer Tierney, who somehow had acquired a handgun and was accompanied by an armed express messenger, left the train and arrived at the scene. The two men fired into the midst of the three outlaws. No one was struck, but the three turned and fled into the woods in a direction different from that taken by May.

The dogged conductor Steele entered the woods in hot pursuit of May and fifty yards later caught up with him. By now May was out of bullets. When he saw Steele approaching, revolver pointed directly at his chest, he threw down his weapon, raised his hands, and surrendered.

Later, when law enforcement officials arrived, May was arrested, taken to Brackenridge, and interrogated. His five companions were never identified or located.

During questioning by lawmen, May claimed he was from Dallas, Texas. Authorities suspected that the name J. D. May was an alias but were never able to coax any pertinent information from their captive. May admitted that he and his companions had planned to rob the passengers and the express car before everything began to go wrong.

A short time after May's arrest, a telegram was sent to the authorities of the San Antonio and Aransas Pass train line, who in turn alerted the US Marshal's Office. On the following day, a US marshal, accompanied by several deputies, arrived at Brackenridge by special train to take custody of the prisoner.

The lawmen arrived just in time to save May from being hanged. Angered by the death of fireman Martin, the engineer

Tierney and conductor Steele, along with other members of the train crew and a few townsfolk, were only moments away from lynching May from the nearest tree.

As a result of further investigation, it was learned that John D. May was indeed an alias for Joe B. Giles of Dallas. Giles was tried, found guilty of attempted train robbery, and hanged in Karnes City on May 25, 1894. It was hoped that the execution of the inept robber would deter others who might consider preying on the railroads, but it was not to be.

In what the local newspapers referred to as "the Great Brackenridge Train Robbery," one man died, five would-be train robbers escaped, and one was captured and executed. In the end, not a single coin was taken.

CHAPTER 21

CANADIAN, TEXAS

April 24, 1894

The botched attempt near Brackenridge on June 1893 was unusual, since by that time the Lone Star State had experienced a number of successful train robberies. What was even more unusual, a second bungled attempt took place on that same night at the small town of Canadian, Texas, located on the south bank of the Canadian River in the northeastern part of the Texas Panhandle and only twenty-five miles from the Oklahoma border. It had been widely rumored that a package containing $25,000 was being transported in the express car.

Moments after the southbound Santa Fe passenger train pulled in at the Canadian depot, a gang of at least six mounted and armed gunmen, reputed to have just arrived in town from the Wichita Mountains in adjacent Oklahoma, rode out from hiding and began firing rifles and revolvers, concentrating on the express car. As the shooting started, Hemphill County sheriff Tom McGee heard the commotion from his office not far away. After strapping on his gun belt and checking the loads in his revolver, McGee hastened to the scene only to be gunned down immediately by the shooters.

On hearing the gunshots, a number of the citizens in the small town armed themselves as well and rushed to the depot, prepared to assist in defending the train from the apparent robbers.

In moments, the townsfolk outnumbered the attackers by a wide margin and began firing into their ranks without mercy. As far as is known, no one was hit. Seeing the tide turn and realizing that their chances of getting into the express car were growing remoter by the second, the thwarted robbers turned their horses and galloped away.

A posse was not long in forming and soon headed off in pursuit of the outlaws. Several days later, four suspects were arrested. Three of them were identified as Jim Harbold, Dan "Jake" McKenzie, and a man known only as Tulsa Jack. All three were known to belong to a train-robbing gang led by the notorious outlaw and train robber Bill Doolin. The fourth captive was not positively identified. The four men were returned to the town of Canadian, where they stood trial for the attempted robbery. Another gang member involved in the attack on the train at Canadian was believed to have been a man named "Red Buck" Waightman, also known to be one of Bill Doolin's henchmen.

Some lawmen were beginning to wonder whether Bill Doolin himself was somehow involved with the attempted robbery. Since he was not present, they suspected he might have at least helped plan the heist.

As preparations were made for the funeral of the late Sheriff McGee, a new development in the attempted train robbery came to the fore. The package alleged to contain $25,000 somehow generated suspicion and was opened. It was found to contain only a bit more than $200. The bills had been stacked atop sheaves of blank paper made to resemble real currency. The investigation into the robbery now took a new turn, and soon the reason behind it was revealed.

As it turned out, an area rancher named George Isaacs had prepared the fake package of money and shipped it to himself at his Hemphill County ranch from Kansas City, Kansas. Isaacs, it was learned, was well acquainted with the train robbers. It was later discovered that Isaacs and the robbers together planned the entire escapade.

Isaacs had planned to have the package stolen by the robbers. A few days later, after the excitement of the event had died down, he intended to file a claim for the full $25,000 from the insurance company. On receiving the amount, Isaacs was to split the money with his cohorts. The rancher had not counted on aggressive townsfolk spoiling the plot; nor did he consider the possibility of a thorough and efficient investigation conducted by the lawmen.

Isaacs was arrested and subsequently charged with fraud and as an accessory in the murder of Sheriff McGee. He was tried, convicted in 1895, and sentenced to life imprisonment at the state penitentiary in Huntsville. According to at least one researcher, Isaacs died in prison after having served a number of years.

Interestingly, another version of Isaacs's fate exists. This one has the rancher escaping from Huntsville and, with the assistance of some family members, fleeing to Mexico, where he lived for several years. Following a significant passage of time, Isaacs allegedly returned to the United States and later settled in Arizona.

To further confuse matters regarding Isaacs, yet another version relates that after having served a considerable portion of his sentence, he was released. It was rumored that he returned to his Texas ranch and lived the life of a recluse until finally passing away. The truth of any of these versions remains elusive.

CHAPTER 22

BLACK JACK KETCHUM

The criminal business of train robbery, it can be argued, attracted men destined for outlaw fame—fearless and daring men with a sense of adventure. It can likewise be argued that the successful train robberies themselves generated the notoriety and recognition associated with many well-known bad men: Frank and Jesse James, Butch Cassidy and the Sundance Kid, Sam Bass, Rube Burrow, and others all held reputations as audacious and successful train robbers.

A lesser-known train robber than the James brothers and Butch Cassidy, but no less effective, was Thomas Edward "Black Jack" Ketchum, regarded by many as a significant and dangerous outlaw scourge of the American West. Ketchum and his brother Sam were well known to lawmen throughout much of Wyoming and Colorado but during most of their criminal careers had never gained the reputation accorded to James, Cassidy, and others.

Thomas Ketchum was born near China Creek on October 31, 1863, in San Saba County in the northern part of the Texas Hill Country. (At least one report says he was born in 1866.) Ketchum's father died when he was only five years old, and his mother, who was blind, passed away when he was ten. Tom's older brother, Green Berry Ketchum, became a successful rancher and breeder of horses in the area. Another brother, Sam, had married and fathered two children. When Tom decided to depart the family fold and travel west to strike out on his own, Sam left his family and joined him. Initially, the two men found work as ranch hands in West Texas and northern New Mexico and participated in a number of cattle drives into Colorado and Wyoming.

By 1892, Tom and Sam had committed themselves to a life of outlawry. Along with several other members of what was referred to as the Black Jack Ketchum Gang, they held up and robbed an Atchison, Topeka and Santa Fe train near Deming, New Mexico. They got away with an estimated $20,000.

Over the next several years, Tom and Sam Ketchum, while occasionally finding work on cattle ranches, preferred instead to pursue their criminal activities, finding them more lucrative and offering more adventure. They and their gang members were responsible for several murders and train robberies.

Oddly, both Tom and Sam were referred to as "Black Jack" at various times, often generating a level of confusion among researchers as to which brother participated in what holdup and to what degree. Though it is suspected both were involved in a number of train robberies together, there is little on record to reveal the truth. At times, both Tom and Sam Ketchum rode with Butch Cassidy, Elzy Lay, Harry Longabaugh, and other members of the Wild Bunch, noted and proficient train robbers themselves. There is little doubt that the brothers learned much about the criminal trade from Cassidy and other gang members. When not riding with the Wild Bunch, Black Jack, sometimes accompanied by his brother and other partners he recruited, went out on his own to indulge in robbing sprees. By late 1895, former Wild Bunch member Harvey "Kid Curry" Logan had become a member of Black Jack's gang.

Of the two brothers, Tom Ketchum was the most recognized and, in the end, generated the most publicity and notoriety. Ketchum was regarded by most who were acquainted with him as "crazy," often exhibiting behavior that was considered bizarre even

Black Jack Ketchum

by the standards of most hardened outlaws. Today, Ketchum would be referred to as a psychopath. The clearly deranged Ketchum was considered far too outrageous, dangerous, and unpredictable even for most of the members of the Wild Bunch, themselves no strangers to violent men, killing, and related activity.

On more than one occasion, Ketchum was observed beating himself over the head with his own revolver and lashing himself across the neck and back with his lariat, self-inflicted punishment for some mistake for which he determined he should be castigated. Once, when a woman he had been seeing decided she wanted nothing more to do with him, Ketchum, in front of gang members, beat himself bloody with the butt of his revolver.

Black Jack Ketchum was also known to drink heavily. Sometimes by himself and other times with companions, he would remain drunk for long periods, the alcohol making him more belligerent than he normally was.

It was just a matter of time before Black Jack Ketchum returned to his home state of Texas to rob a train.

CHAPTER 23

LOZIER STATION, TEXAS

May 14, 1897

On May 14, 1897, Thomas "Black Jack" Ketchum, along with two unidentified companions, robbed a Southern Pacific train near the remote and lonely Lozier Station in the Big Bend Country of West Texas, 250 straight-line miles west of San Antonio. Though unidentified, one of Ketchum's partners was believed by many to be Ben Kilpatrick, who had previous train-robbing experience as a member of the Wild Bunch. Years later, Kilpatrick would return to that part of West Texas to attempt another robbery of this same train. It would prove his last.

At 2:00 a.m. on May 10, the Southern Pacific *Sunset Limited* made an emergency stop at the unmanned Lozier siding. The train had pulled out of Del Rio near the Mexican border less than an hour earlier and was westbound for El Paso. Several minutes after leaving Del Rio, the engineer, a man named Freese, told the conductor, named Burns, that the train was running erratically. Since the next station down the line was Lozier, Freese recommended they stop there to determine the problem. After pulling into the station, Freese and the conductor examined the train in an attempt to locate the disturbance. As the men were thus occupied, the fireman topped off the water tank from the supply positioned next to the tracks.

The express car was several dozen yards behind the engine and coal tender and at least one passenger car. Wells Fargo messenger

Henry Boyce was in the final stages of conducting an inventory of the shipment that had been placed on board at Del Rio. The shipment consisted of over $90,000 in paper currency and a bit more than $6,000 in silver coins. Boyce had carefully placed the shipment in the safe, which he then closed and locked.

Engineer Freese descended from the cab in the dark, then walked around the locomotive and examined it, trying to find the source of the problem. He was accompanied by conductor Burns. As the two went about their inspection, three men observed their movements from the deep shadows of the station building a short distance away. One of the men was Black Jack Ketchum. By this time, Ketchum was a well-known and wanted outlaw who had made his reputation as a train robber in Colorado and Wyoming. Because of continual scrapes with the law in those states, as well as the fact that he was heavily pursued, Ketchum had drifted south with his gang into Texas, where he was less known.

It took Freese and Burns an hour to detect and correct the problem with the engine. Shortly after climbing back into the locomotive, the engineer gave the signal to proceed, and the train was under way. As the train began the slow departure from the station, before it picked up momentum, the outlaws struck. Ketchum, carrying a knapsack and a rifle, and one of his partners dashed from their hiding place and leaped onto one of the railroad cars. The two men climbed the ladder to the roof and made their way over several more cars toward the engine.

As Ketchum and his companion were making their way forward, the outlaw remaining behind cut the telegraph wire that connected this station to others down the line. This done, he dashed several dozen yards away and down into a shallow draw, where the bandits' horses had been hobbled. After removing the fetters, the outlaw mounted his own and led the other two out of the draw and along the tracks behind the train.

By the time the train had traveled five miles, Ketchum and his companion had reached the coal tender, crossed it, and jumped down into the cab of the locomotive. Ketchum pointed his rifle at engineer Freese and ordered him to stop the train. The second outlaw trained his gun on conductor Burns, who was accompanying Freese in the cab, along with the fireman, Bochat. When the train had come to a stop, Ketchum forced Freese, Burns, and Bochat out of the cab and instructed them to stand next to the tracks. Ketchum descended the cab and ordered Freese to take him to the express car. Freese led the way. Ketchum followed, the tip of his rifle barrel just inches from Freese's head.

On reaching the express car, pointed out by Freese, Ketchum banged on the door with the butt of his rifle and demanded that messenger Boyce open it. The outlaw received no response. Twice more Ketchum called out, only to be greeted with silence. Growing annoyed and angry, Ketchum crawled beneath the express car, cocked his rifle, and fired a round up through the wooden floor. Believing he had finally secured Boyce's attention, he yelled for the messenger to open the door or he would shoot Freese through the head.

Again, Ketchum received no response from Boyce. Concerned about the potential fate of the engineer, fireman Bochat, who had been watching from his position near the locomotive, tentatively approached the express car and begged Boyce to open the door. He explained that Ketchum was quite serious relative to his threat to kill the engineer if he did not. After several tense seconds, Ketchum and the railroad employees could hear the inside latches being released. A moment later, the express car door slid open, and Boyce stepped up to the opening with his hands raised. Ketchum pulled his revolver from its holster, pointed it at Boyce, and ordered him to step to the rear of the car. This done, Ketchum climbed in.

Once inside the express car, Ketchum ordered Boyce to open the safe. When Boyce said that he did not know the combination, Ketchum placed the barrel of his rifle against the messenger's neck. Nervous and shaking, Boyce explained that the only person who knew the combination was the relief messenger in El Paso; the procedure was now railroad company policy.

Angered even more by this revelation, Ketchum knocked Boyce to the floor. From his own coat pocket, the outlaw withdrew four sticks of dynamite, tied together in a bundle. Setting down his rifle, he knelt in front of the safe, attached the explosives to the heavy metal door, and lit the fuse. Rising, he approached Boyce, tossed him from the express car, and leaped to the ground after him. As the dynamite fuse burned, Ketchum ran for the shelter of some nearby rocks. As he did, he warned Freese, Burns, Bochat, and Boyce to take cover.

A few seconds later, the surrounding desert vibrated with the sound of the huge explosion, and smoke billowed out of the opening of the express car. When it cleared, Ketchum reentered the car. He found the door to the safe completely blown away but the contents within remarkably undisturbed.

Ketchum filled his knapsack and saddlebags with the silver coins. He checked his watch and noted that ninety minutes had passed since the train had pulled away from the Lozier station. A moment later, the third outlaw arrived with the horses. After tying the coin-filled knapsack behind his saddle, the always unpredictable Ketchum bade a polite good-bye to Freese, Burns, Bochat, and Boyce and, along with his two companions, rode away toward the southwest in the direction of the Chisos Mountains. Although he was $6,000 richer in coins, Ketchum had missed the $90,000 in currency being transported in the car.

As Ketchum and his gang disappeared into the desert darkness, Freese raced back to the engine and in a short time had the train barreling toward the next stop, Sanderson. On pulling into the station, conductor Burns leaped out of the cab and informed the agent of what had happened at Lozier. He instructed him to telegraph news of the robbery to Southern Pacific Railroad authorities in El Paso immediately.

By the time the sun came up, Texas Ranger captain John R. Hughes had received news of the robbery. From the Ranger encampment at Ysleta, some twenty miles downriver from El Paso, Hughes handpicked a platoon of fifteen Rangers, armed them, and supplied them with provisions to last at least a week. After assembling a string of strong and trail-hardened mounts, the Rangers set out toward the robbery site.

When the Texas Ranger contingent rode up to the scene of the robbery, they found enough signs to indicate that the robbers had fled toward the southwest. After following the tracks for a short distance, however, the Rangers lost them. For several days, Hughes and company searched the rugged, arid country just south

John Hughes

of the robbery site but to no avail—they were unable to pick up the trail of the bandits. On the fourth day, as they were circling a potential area, one of the Rangers came across the tracks of three horses heading southwestward. The Rangers followed the trail for a few miles but lost it again, this time when it crossed a granite outcrop. For another full week, the Rangers crisscrossed the area in hopes of relocating the tracks of the outlaws but were unsuccessful. Captain Hughes finally called a halt to the search and returned with his charges to Ysleta.

After fleeing from the robbery site, Ketchum and his companions rode hard for two days and nights, stopping only to water and rest the horses. On the morning of the third day of flight, the gang had made its way deep into the remote and barely accessible reaches of the Big Bend Country not far from the Mexican border. Two more days of riding through dark, narrow canyons and across rugged, rocky ridges brought them to their planned destination: the isolated ranch of the Reagan brothers in Reagan Canyon.

The relationship between the four Reagan brothers and the outlaw Black Jack Ketchum was long-standing. The ranchers agreed to allow Ketchum and his gang to hide out in the area for a few days. As the train robbers unsaddled their horses, one of the ranch hands obliterated their tracks by driving a herd of cattle over them.

Ketchum was concerned that the Texas Rangers would be searching for them and might be closing in on their hideout. It was just a matter of time, he reasoned, before they arrived. Not wanting to be caught with the $6,000 in silver coins and fearing that if he continued to transport them in his saddlebags they would slow him down, Ketchum decided to cache the loot on the ranch. After giving the Reagan brothers $200 worth of coins, Ketchum stuffed the remaining loot into his knapsack and carried it to a cave he had located earlier a short distance north of Reagan Canyon. The next day, the three outlaws rode away, intending to return at some future date and retrieve the treasure. None of them could have realized that they would never see that part of Texas again.

Ketchum decided it was in his best interest to put as much distance as possible between himself and the Texas Rangers, so he traveled to Colorado. Once settled into the Rocky Mountain state, the outlaw lost no time in returning to robbing trains.

On September 3, 1897, Ketchum and his gang robbed a Colorado and Southern train, making off with $3,500. On July 11, 1899, the gang struck again, robbing the same train and taking $70,000 in gold coins. It was to be the last successful robbery undertaken by Ketchum.

Following the July 11 robbery, Huerfano County, Colorado, sheriff Farr assembled a posse consisting of nine men experienced in tracking and fighting. They were accompanied by two railroad detectives. A few days later, the posse caught up with the robbers, and a gunfight ensued. Two members of the gang were killed, and Black Jack's brother, Sam, was wounded. Black Jack, along with Bill Franks and another man named McGinnis, escaped.

Sam Ketchum was arrested. While awaiting trial in a Santa Fe, New Mexico, jail, he contracted blood poisoning, presumably from his wound, and died. Franks was killed in San Angelo, Texas, in 1901. McGinnis was later captured, tried, and sentenced to the New Mexico penitentiary. He was pardoned in 1906.

Though his gang had been decimated, and he had suffered significant failure, Thomas "Black Jack" Ketchum was more determined than ever to return to robbing trains. His next attempt turned out to be his last.

CHAPTER 24

THE ARREST AND EXECUTION OF TOM "BLACK JACK" KETCHUM

On April 16, 1899, Black Jack Ketchum was in New Mexico, safe from pursuit by Texas lawmen. Alone, he had decided to rob the Colorado and Southern train for the third time near Folsom, New Mexico.

It is not clear why Ketchum was not in the company of gang members. The historical record shows that train robberies executed by a single outlaw were rarely successful. After spending the night in a nearby cave, Ketchum rode to the railroad station at Folsom, turned his horse loose, boarded the train from the blind side of the baggage car, and made his way to the coal tender.

After the train had traveled about three miles from the station, Ketchum jumped into the locomotive cab from the coal tender to the surprise of the engineer and ordered the train stopped. The outlaw's plan was to disconnect the express and mail cars from the rest of the train and have the engineer proceed another mile up the track. There, the train was to be stopped once more, and Ketchum would make his way to the express and mail cars, where he intended to retrieve any money there. The train robber erred, however, in determining the location for the train to stop. It was on a tight curve, which left the train in a cramped position and, as it turned out, made it impossible to uncouple the cars.

After the train stopped, Ketchum climbed down from the cab and made his way to the cars he had targeted. Meeting with little to no resistance, he opened the door to the express car and climbed in. Some have recorded that the always-volatile Ketchum, after entering the car, shot the express messenger in the jaw. Others say this did not happen.

The conductor, Frank Harrington, had lost his patience with train robbers. His train had already been robbed three times, and he was determined it would not happen again. Noting that only one robber seemed to be involved in this attempt, Harrington grabbed a shotgun and went after Ketchum.

The conductor found the robber inside the baggage car, pointed his weapon at him, and made his presence known. Reflexively, Ketchum got off a hurried shot at the conductor, barely missing him. (One report states that the conductor was struck by the bullet.) At about the same time, Harrington fired a barrel from the scattergun he was carrying, the load of buckshot striking Ketchum in the left elbow, destroying the lower arm and nearly severing it from the upper. The impact knocked the outlaw out of the express car and onto the ground. Harrington shouted for the engineer to get the train moving as fast as possible.

Bleeding heavily, Ketchum ran toward his horse. As he later explained to his interrogators, he tried a dozen times to climb into the saddle but was too weak to manage. Dizzy from the effort, he collapsed to the ground and decided to wait for the inevitable posse to arrive.

The engineer stopped the Colorado and Southern train at every station he came to, each time having telegrams sent to various law enforcement agencies reporting the robbery and advising them to be on the lookout for a badly wounded man who was likely still near the scene of the attempted holdup. A short time later, the train pulled into the station at Clayton, New Mexico, where the engineer reported the attempted holdup to the sheriff. A posse was formed and raced back to the robbery site but found no sign of Ketchum.

Fearing that he would bleed to death from his wound, Ketchum had managed to flag down another train. When the train stopped, the brakeman climbed down from the cab and approached the apparently injured stranger. As the brakeman neared, Ketchum drew his revolver and pointed it at him. The conductor was quoted as saying, "We just came to help you, but if this is the way you feel we will go and leave you."

The weakening Ketchum lowered his weapon and told the brakeman that he was "all done," and to "take me in." He was placed in the caboose, laid down on a cot, and, with a guard stationed next to him, was carried into Folsom. He was later placed under arrest by Union County sheriff Saturnino Pinard.

At his arrest, Ketchum gave his name as Frank Stevens. (At least one writer claimed that the name he gave was George Stevens.) His wound was patched up as well as could be managed. Forty-two shotgun pellets were removed from the damaged arm. Later, Ketchum was taken to the San Rafael Hospital at Trinidad, Colorado, where his mangled arm was amputated.

As the investigation proceeded, authorities soon learned that the name Stevens was an alias and that the man who sat before them was none other than the notorious train robber Black Jack Ketchum, a man who had managed to elude New Mexico lawmen for a long time. They also learned that Ketchum was wanted in four other states for murder, bank robbery, train robbery, and other crimes. When he was well enough to travel, Ketchum was transported to Santa Fe for a time for "safekeeping."

While Black Jack Ketchum was in custody in Santa Fe, detectives and other officials arrived to question him about the robbery of the Southern Pacific *Sunset Limited* near Lozier Station in West Texas. Ketchum admitted his role in the robbery and provided details.

Ketchum also described his long flight southwestward into the arid Big Bend Country and hiding out at the Reagan brothers' ranch for a few days. Ketchum even confessed to caching the knapsack filled with silver coins in a remote cave located on the ranch. The coins, he informed them, were still there because he had not had an opportunity to return for them, and the two companions who had accompanied him at the time, he claimed, were dead. When the lawmen asked for specific directions to the cave, Ketchum refused to give them any.

The former Texan and now one-armed Black Jack Ketchum was returned to Clayton, New Mexico, where he was formally charged. He was tried, found guilty, and sentenced to be hanged. Back in his jail cell, Ketchum received an opportunity to make a confession to a priest. Instead he told the holy man, "I'm gonna die as I've lived. And you ain't gonna change me in a few minutes." Then he smiled and said, "Have someone play a fiddle when I swing off." The priest was sent on his way.

At 8:00 a.m. on April 26, 1901, Thomas "Black Jack" Ketchum was marched to the gallows. He was manacled, and a heavy steel belt encircled his waist. His left arm was cuffed to the belt, and his legs were linked together with a short length of chain. He was also surrounded by several armed lawmen, rifles at the ready. The reason for applying these seemingly unnecessary precautions to a one-armed, heavily shackled prisoner related to a rumor circulating throughout Clayton the previous day that some of Ketchum's gang members might arrive to try to free him.

Within minutes after Ketchum had ascended the steps to the gallows, a rope was placed around his neck and a black hood fitted over his head. The hood was pinned to his shirt.

As he was being readied for execution, Ketchum taunted his captors, stating, "Hurry up, boys, get this over with." The outlaw was also credited with saying, "I'll be in hell before you start breakfast, boys!" Following some final adjustments to the noose, Ketchum yelled, "Let 'er rip!"

Clayton sheriff Garcia needed two hatchet blows to sever the rope that released the trapdoor on which Ketchum stood. As it swung open, Ketchum dropped through the opening, his body plummeting toward the ground. When it suddenly reached the end of the length of rope, the head snapped from the torso. The head remained inside the black hood. One writer said the only thing keeping it from rolling away was the fact that the hood was pinned to the shirt. This seems unlikely—if the force was strong enough to tear the head from the body, it surely would have torn the hood away from the shirt. Another writer wrote that the body separated from the head and then the head fell on top of the body after it swung loose from the rope. Onlookers screamed. Photographs were then taken of the head and the decapitated body. Ketchum was later buried in the new Clayton cemetery.

Such decapitations were unheard of in formal executions of the time. A number of explanations for this unusual occurrence have been offered, including (1) the gallows was too high, and the speed attained by the body while falling was sufficient to separate it from the head; (2) the noose was too tight; and/or (3) the rope was too thin for such a heavy man and thus cut through flesh and bone. Some even suggested the decapitation was purposeful, though no evidence for such was ever advanced.

Black Jack Ketchum's outlaw life has been told and retold in books, articles, and film. Lacking the charm and glamour of other notorious outlaws and train robbers of the day, such as Butch Cassidy, Jesse James, and others, Ketchum is simply regarded by most researchers as a crazed robber and killer with few, if any, redeeming qualities. Black Jack was the only man subjected to capital punishment in the state of New Mexico for "felonious assault upon a railway train."

Black Jack Ketchum had a long and colorful life journey after leaving his home in San Saba County, Texas. His travels took him throughout much of the American West, his ambitions carrying him from one criminal escapade to another.

The silver coins Black Jack Ketchum took from the Southern Pacific Railroad near Lozier, Texas, and cached in a remote cave in southwestern Texas are still searched for to this day.

CHAPTER 25

McNEILL, TEXAS
October 12, 1897

The citizens of McNeill had long since recovered from the train robbery that had taken place in their town on May 18, 1887. Convinced that lightning would not strike twice in the same place, they were unprepared for the autumn robbery of an International and Great Northern (I&GN) train.

As the I&GN passenger train pulled away from the McNeill station at 5:30 p.m., two men ran from their hiding place and jumped aboard the rear platform of the last passenger coach. There they waited patiently until the time was right. The train had only traveled a few miles from McNeill when the conductor, an affable gentleman named Thomas Healy, opened the car door, stepped out onto the platform, and asked the men for their tickets.

Both travelers reached into their pockets, but instead of retrieving tickets, they withdrew revolvers, which they pointed at Healy. The conductor paused for only a second or two, then wheeled and raced back through the door and down the aisle of the passenger coach. When he was halfway through the car, one of the men on the platform fired a shot, the bullet striking Healy in the right arm and dropping him to the floor.

A second later, one of the newcomers stepped into the car and pulled the bell cord, a signal for the engineer to stop the train. As the train slowed, two additional men, their faces hidden by masks, stepped from their hiding place among some nearby trees and

107

approached the passenger car, revolvers in hand. As they neared the coach, they fired their weapons into it, forcing the commuters to duck for shelter between the seats. The fusillade was intended to send a message to the passengers that no resistance would be tolerated. The shirt collar of one passenger was ripped by a bullet, and another passenger was struck in the hand.

Once all the bandits had boarded the train, they opened the doors of the three passenger coaches so that they could see down the aisles. One bandit stood at each end of the line of passenger cars, pointing his weapon at the occupants. The remaining two walked down the tracks to the express car.

On arriving at the express car, the robbers convinced the messenger to open the door or suffer the consequences. When he complied, the outlaws entered and located the safe, which was locked. Holding a gun to the head of the messenger, they ordered him to open it, but the frightened man explained that he did not have the combination. Frustrated, the two bandits left the express car and returned to the passenger coaches. Once there, they passed down the aisles taking money, watches, jewelry, and other valuables from the occupants.

When convinced that they had harvested all that was possible, the robbers returned to the locomotive, uncoupled it from the tender, climbed into the cab, and proceeded down the tracks.

After they had traveled several miles, the robbers slowed the locomotive so that they could leap from it. After gathering themselves, they watched as the steam engine disappeared into the distance. Eventually, the fire abated, the boiler ran out of steam, and the engine stopped near the town of Duval.

Aside from the man with the wounded hand, none of the other commuters were injured. Though the bandits were unable to breach the safe, they collected a significant amount of money and valuables from the passengers before escaping. The robbers have never been identified, and the case was never solved.

CHAPTER 26

TEMPLE, TEXAS

June 10, 1898

Of the twenty-seven train robberies that took place in Texas between 1878 and 1921, a handful were unsuccessful due to a variety of factors. Inexperience was responsible in at least one case, and sometimes circumstances existed that were beyond the would-be robbers' control.

Yet another botched train robbery took place at a location west of Temple on June 10, 1898, with an unfortunate result. The robbers failed in their bid to enter and steal the money from the express car, but during the robbery attempt shots were fired, and the fireman was killed.

Information on the 1898 Temple train robbery is sparse. Local newspapers gave the event very little coverage, and a published account of the attempted robbery appeared, oddly, in the June 11 issue of the *Sacramento Daily Union*. As far as can be discerned, not a single Texas newspaper reported on the event in any depth.

According to the Sacramento paper, a San Angelo–bound Santa Fe Railroad passenger train was flagged down by four armed men around midnight. The train pulled to a stop at a siding shortly after departing Temple. At least two of the would-be robbers stepped out of hiding, approached the locomotive, and climbed into the cab. There, they held the engineer and fireman at gunpoint and ordered the former to accompany them to the express car, which he was to detach from the rest of the train. The outlaws then wanted the engineer to pull the train and the trailing express car another mile or two farther up the track where it was to be robbed. The engineer stubbornly refused to comply with the order and, despite having two revolvers leveled at him, decided to put up a fight. During the ensuing scuffle inside the cab, the fireman was shot and later died.

With the robbery not proceeding according to plan, the four outlaws panicked, abruptly discarded all attempts to enter the express car, and rode away.

Despite what was reported to the local law enforcement authorities and to the railroad company, and despite the death of the fireman at the hands of the inept robbers, Santa Fe Railroad officials insisted they had never been advised of the robbery attempt and, for reasons known only to them, even denied that it ever happened.

A somewhat belated search for the robbers was undertaken by local law enforcement authorities. By the time a posse arrived at the scene of the attempted train robbery several days later, however, any sign that may have suggested the direction of the outlaws' flight had long since been obliterated. Had they been apprehended, a charge of murder would have been filed against them. A half-hearted investigation ensued, but no significant evidence was ever found, and the results were unsuccessful. None of the would-be bandits were ever identified.

CHAPTER 27

COLEMAN, TEXAS

June 10, 1898

The occurrence of two train robberies on the same day was rare in Texas as well as throughout the nation. The same newspaper that reported the June 10, 1898, Temple train robbery also filed an article related to a second heist that took place within one hour of the other in Coleman, 150 miles northwest of Temple. As with the Temple train robbery, information was scarce.

At 1:00 a.m., a Santa Fe passenger train arrived at the Coleman station and pulled to a stop. The fireman, Lee Johnson, jumped down from the train to throw a switch when he was approached by four men who walked out of the darkness carrying shotguns. When Johnson turned to address the men he found himself staring into the barrels of their weapons. At gunpoint, fireman Johnson was forced to lead the robbers to the express car. There, one of the gang members hammered on the door, but the messenger inside refused to open it. Not to be denied, the robbers began firing their weapons through the wooden door.

A claim agent named Buchan was a passenger on the train. When it pulled to a stop, he climbed out of the car and onto the station platform. While he was standing there, he observed fireman Johnson being escorted toward the express car by the four gunmen. It became clear to Buchan that a robbery was in progress. The claim agent pulled a revolver from beneath his coat and fired at the gang, his bullet striking one of the robbers in the leg. The other three bandits responded by firing back at Buchan and anyone else they considered a target. Fireman Johnson, who was standing next to the outlaws, was struck twice, with both bullets "going through the bowels." He died several hours later.

Nearing panic, the would-be robbers, thwarted from harvesting any money or anything else of value, as well as being subjected to gunfire, fled the scene. On foot, they raced to their horses, mounted up, and rode away into the night. Several posses were formed, all setting out in pursuit of the outlaws.

Searches were conducted over the next several days, and in time three men were arrested: Pierce Keaton, Brad Newman, and Bill Taylor. Jeff Taylor, Bill's brother, managed to elude the lawmen and was never apprehended. The Santa Fe Railroad had offered a $600 reward for the capture of the men.

While interrogating the prisoners, lawmen identified Newman as the leader of the gang. It was learned that these same men had been active robbing banks in and around Temple. It was also suspected that the gang had been involved in earlier train robberies in Texas where the participants were never identified, but nothing was ever proven.

With the exchange of gunfire during the Coleman train robbery, outlaw Newman had been wounded in the arm, and Buchan had struck Keaton in the leg. It was also learned that Keaton fired the shots that were responsible for the death of fireman Johnson.

Brad Newman and Bill Taylor were tried, found guilty, and sentenced to long terms in prison. Keaton was convicted of killing Johnson and sentenced to prison for life. In 1915 he was paroled and went to live in Bisbee, Arizona. He died in 1931.

CHAPTER 28

BASSETT, TEXAS

December 14, 1900

Of all the train robberies that took place in Texas, as well as throughout the United States, most were solved relative to determining the identities of those involved and what sort of loot had been targeted. In a significant percentage of these robberies, the outlaws were apprehended, and in many cases some or all of the stolen money was recovered.

A train robbery that occurred on a northbound Cotton Belt express train between Bassett and Texarkana, in December 1900 turned out to be one of the most unusual ever undertaken in Texas, or anywhere else for that matter. In addition, it was fraught with mystery. To this day, it has not been solved, and the robbers were never caught.

The mystery started when the Cotton Belt train pulled out of the station at Bassett on December 14, 1900. Bassett was and is a tiny community located fourteen miles south of DeKalb in Bowie County. The train had not gone far when the engineer suddenly realized that the passenger coaches had somehow become uncoupled and remained back at the station. In addition, the mail car and express car had also been uncoupled from the rest of the train. The engineer stopped the train and then backed the locomotive all the way to the station. On returning, the crew got busy and recoupled all the cars. Once this was done to the satisfaction of the engineer, the train proceeded on to Texarkana.

The train had traveled approximately ten miles when the engineer realized that the cars had somehow become uncoupled again, this time during transit. The train was stopped, and, as before, the crew bent to the task of recoupling the cars. A thorough examination was undertaken by the engineer and the fireman, but they could find no explanation for the unusual occurrence. Two uncouplings of the same cars within so short a time was a problem never before encountered by the engineer or any of the crew members. Ultimately satisfied that everything was in order, the engineer climbed back into the locomotive and proceeded on toward Texarkana.

Before the Cotton Belt train reached its destination, however, the cars had become uncoupled for yet a third time. After stopping the train and recoupling the cars once more, the train crew instigated another search for the cause of the problem but found no evidence of tampering whatsoever. On arriving at the Texarkana station, another examination was conducted, but once again the crew could not determine the cause of the uncouplings.

Shortly after the train pulled to a stop at Texarkana, a transfer clerk for the Railway Mail Service walked over to the mail car to conduct business with the mail clerk, John N. Dennis. The clerk thought it was strange, even suspicious, when there was no response to his knock on the mail car door. He returned to the station at once and alerted nearby postal officials, who arrived back at the mail car a few minutes later. After prying open the car door, the officials entered and were surprised to find Dennis lying on the floor, unconscious from an apparent heavy blow to the head. Not far from Dennis, the officials spotted several mail bags that had been torn open and the contents removed.

The postal officials attempted to revive Dennis, but his injury was so severe that he had to be transported to a nearby hospital. Hours later, when he recovered, he told the investigators what had happened. Dennis's explanation added more confusion and intrigue to the situation.

Dennis stated that after collecting the mail at the Bassett station, he carried the bags to the mail car, unlocked the door, tossed the bags inside, and climbed in, only to find two armed men waiting for him. As Dennis turned back toward the open door to shout an alarm, he was struck across the back of his head with a large shovel and knocked unconscious. He was unaware of anything that had taken place in the mail car afterward. The next thing he knew he was being revived at a hospital.

When the Cotton Belt railroad company was alerted to the perplexing robbery, it sent its own inspectors to the mail car to conduct a thorough investigation. One of the first problems to deal with was determining how anyone could have possibly entered the locked car. Dennis, a reliable employee, had made certain the door was fastened before walking over to the station to retrieve the mail. In addition, no access was available through the windows as they were protected by iron bars.

As one of the investigators was examining the inside of the mail car, he spotted a small trap door centered at one end. It was the first time he had ever seen one in a mail car. Moments later, he found another at the opposite end of the car. When he approached the engineer and inquired about the trap doors, he learned that they existed to provide access to a crank that could be employed to uncouple cars in case of an emergency. There were no locks or latches on the trapdoors, so they could be opened from inside or outside the car. The trapdoor was designed to be large enough for a man to insert his arm and reach down to the crank.

The trap doors were rarely used by the crewmen and had been installed only as a precaution. During the investigation, however, the officials determined that it was possible that a person of small stature could enter and leave through the same opening.

Ultimately, it was determined that the two men Dennis encountered in the mail car had obtained entrance through one or both of the trapdoor openings. Once the train was in motion, the postal inspectors reasoned that the bandits had reached back through the trapdoors to uncouple the cars. It was also assumed that during the third uncoupling of the cars during the run from Bassett to Texarkana, the resourceful outlaws had slipped out of the same openings and made their escape unnoticed.

The mysterious train robbers were never caught or identified, and none of the stolen mail was ever recovered. Today, the Bassett train robbery is classified as an unsolved crime.

CHAPTER 29

EYLAU SIDING, TEXAS

September 3, 1901

What some writers have described as the perfect railroad holdup took place on September 3, 1901, near Eylau Siding in Bowie County, located five miles southwest of Texarkana. The reason for such praise was likely the fact that one or more of the robbers had once been employed by a railroad, giving rise to a common observation that "railroaders make the best train robbers." Indeed, evidence has suggested that this was the case with the Eylau Siding robbery. Train robbery researcher and author Richard Patterson once wrote, "In more than half the outlaw gangs that preyed on express and railway mail cars during the 1880s and 1890s, you probably could have found at least one former railroader."

The southbound Cotton Belt train departed the Texarkana station at 9:25 p.m. The trip was smooth and trouble-free until the train was scheduled to stop at a junction with the Texas and Pacific tracks four miles away. As soon as the train pulled to a stop, six men, all armed with revolvers and rifles and wearing masks, appeared out of the shadows and climbed into the locomotive cab. There, they relieved the engineer and fireman and took control of the train.

While the engineer, a man named Henderson, and the fireman were held at gunpoint, the rest of the robbers walked down the tracks to the mail and express cars. On arriving, they uncoupled

117

them from the rest of the train. The outlaws then broke into the express car, located the safe, attached a charge of dynamite to it, and blew it open. This done, they stuffed the contents into two large canvas bags. Having accomplished this segment of the robbery to their satisfaction, the outlaws returned to the locomotive. Engineer Henderson, again at gunpoint, was ordered to deliver the engine to the siding at the small community of Eylau, a short distance down the track.

During the trip to the siding, one of the outlaws became engaged in a conversation with Henderson. As the robber spoke, it became clear to the engineer that the man possessed some significant railroad experience, as he was well versed in the jargon and technique peculiar to railroaders. The outlaw also appeared quite intimate with the functions of all the knobs and levers normally at the disposal of the engineer.

On arriving at the siding, Henderson was ordered off the train. The robbers kept the fireman on board to feed fuel and maintain the boiler. Once Henderson was on the ground, the outlaw at the controls advanced the locomotive on down the track.

Henderson made his way on foot in the opposite direction to a utility shack. There, he procured a handcart and returned the way he had just come, hoping to catch up to and retrieve his locomotive. He came upon it eight miles away, where it had been stopped along a section of the railroad tracks bordered by a dense forest. Henderson could find no tracks of the robbers; nor could he determine which direction they had traveled after leaving the train. In fact, no trace of the outlaws was ever found, and the contents of the pillaged safe were never recovered.

When railroad officials were interviewed days later about the robbery, they described it as the perfect holdup. Today, Eylau is officially designated as a Texas ghost town.

CHAPTER 30

BEN KILPATRICK

Ben Kilpatrick came into this world on January 5, 1874, in Coleman County, Texas, the third of nine children begat by George Washington Kilpatrick and his wife, Mary. The elder Kilpatrick had migrated to Texas from Tennessee and established a farm. But like many young men possessing a lust for adventure and a desire to see what lay beyond the horizon, young Ben was not content with what he regarded as the drudgery of farmwork.

At the first opportunity, Ben Kilpatrick left home and found work on area cattle ranches. Feeding his hunger to see more of the country, he traveled west, eventually meeting up with noted outlaws and train robbers Tom "Black Jack" Ketchum, his brother Sam, and Will Carver. Kilpatrick found something in these men that appealed to him, and he was bound to follow them. From that time on, life outside the law remained Kilpatrick's chosen path. Learning his lessons well from some of the best, he went on to become known as one of the most prolific train robbers in the American West.

Kilpatrick, nicknamed "the Tall Texan," stood six feet, two inches at a time when a man's average height was around five feet, seven inches. He had a light complexion, and his unusual eyes were described as yellow with violet spots. Kilpatrick was skilled in the use of the handgun and described as "fearless." It was not long before he was accepted as a member of the Black Jack Ketchum Gang, which at the time was focused on robbing trains in New Mexico.

Following his release from prison, having served time for horse theft, Butch Cassidy, along with his friend Elzy Lay, formed a gang that was to become known as the Wild Bunch. After each criminal act they undertook, the gang members retreated to a remote hideout in Utah known as Robbers Roost. Word of the location became known to a number of outlaws. It was also known

Ben Kilpatrick

to lawmen, but none dared venture into these canyons for fear they would never come out.

Following a failed train robbery in New Mexico, Ben Kilpatrick traveled to Robbers Roost, made friends with outlaw Elzy Lay, and was soon regarded as a member of the Wild Bunch. In addition to Cassidy and Lay, other members of the gang at various times included Harry Longabaugh (the Sundance Kid), Harvey Logan, Kid Curry, Will Carver, and Bob Meeks. Additional members of the gang from time to time were the brothers Black Jack and Sam Ketchum.

The Wild Bunch soon gained a reputation as the most successful and feared train-robbing gang in American history. While Kilpatrick spent time off and on with the Wild Bunch, it is not clear to what extent he was directly involved in train robberies that included Cassidy and Longabaugh. Kilpatrick spent most of his time in the Wild Bunch with Kid Curry.

It is known for certain that on August 20, 1900, Kilpatrick, along with Cassidy, Longabaugh, Logan, and Carver, successfully held up the Union Pacific train at Tipton, Wyoming, and made off with over $32,000. The following year, the gang took $65,000 during the robbery of a Great Northern train near Wagner, Montana. Rewards for the members of the Wild Bunch were offered, and wanted posters for each were tacked up throughout the West. For his part, Kilpatrick decided it was time to depart Wyoming.

On April 2, 1901, Kilpatrick and Will Carver rode into Sonora, Texas. Most researchers suspect the two men were planning a train robbery. While in Sonora, they encountered Sheriff Elijah Bryant and a handful of deputies. Bryant recognized Kilpatrick and Carver from wanted posters, and when the sheriff attempted to arrest the two men, a shootout ensued. Carver was killed, and Kilpatrick escaped.

Kilpatrick fled to St. Louis, Missouri, with a female companion, Laura Bullion, a former companion of Carver's. According to most published information on Bullion, she was born in Knickerbocker, Texas, in 1876 (some accounts claim 1873, and one lists 1887). In recent years a document surfaced that offers evidence that she may have been born in Palarm Township in Faulkner County, Arkansas.

Her father, Henry Bullion, was an American Indian and had a brief career as an outlaw. Henry Bullion was a criminal associate of Will Carver and Ben Kilpatrick.

Laura Bullion

For a time, Bullion consorted with members of the Wild Bunch, mostly as a prostitute and partner to Kid Curry, Black Jack Ketchum, and the Sundance Kid. Her nickname among members of the Wild Bunch was "Della Rose."

Kilpatrick and Bullion had not been in St. Louis long when the two were arrested on November 8, 1901. Kilpatrick was tried and found guilty of train robbery and sentenced to the federal penitentiary in Atlanta, Georgia, for fifteen years. Bullion was sentenced to five years at the Missouri State Penitentiary. She was released after serving three and a half years.

Following her release from prison, Bullion moved to Memphis, Tennessee, where she told people her name was Freda Bullion Lincoln and that she was the war widow of a man named Maurice Lincoln. She made her living as a seamstress and later as a drapery maker. As far as is known, for the remainder of her life she never encountered Kilpatrick again. By the 1940s, she had difficulty finding work and was penniless. She died of heart disease in 1961 and was buried in the Memorial Park Cemetery in Memphis.

Kilpatrick was released from prison on June 11, 1911, after serving ten years. Once out of prison, the Tall Texan returned immediately to his criminal ways and engaged in a number of train robberies in the area of Memphis. It is unclear whether Kilpatrick was aware that Laura Bullion was living in Memphis at the time.

Following the spate of robberies, Tennessee law enforcement authorities began to close in, and Kilpatrick felt it prudent to move on to some place where he was less well known. He decided it was time to return to Texas. Once there, he lost no time in directing his attention to planning another train robbery, and he focused on the Southern Pacific *Sunset Limited* that ran along a remote stretch of railroad track in the West Texas desert.

CHAPTER 31

SANDERSON, TEXAS
March 13, 1912

On returning to Texas, the veteran train robber Ben Kilpatrick set his sights on pulling a heist in the Lone Star State. Experienced in this specialized type of outlaw activity, Kilpatrick saw some logic in selecting a train that could be stopped in a remote area, far from curious and possibly armed onlookers. Further, his keen under-standing of how railroads operated led him to identify and select a train that carried a minimum of crew members.

Since nearly all his former train-robbing companions were either dead or scattered, Kilpatrick picked as his new partner a man named Ole Hobek. Kilpatrick and Hobek became friends while in prison. After scouting the area and familiarizing himself with train schedules, Kilpatrick selected the Southern Pacific *Sunset Limited* as his target, and he decided on a remote location in West Texas to conduct the holdup. The *Sunset Limited* was, in fact, the same train robbed in 1897 by Kilpatrick's friend Black Jack Ketchum. Most researchers believe that Kilpatrick was one of the robbers who accompanied Ketchum on that job. If that's true, Kilpatrick was already familiar with the location, as well as real and potential escape routes.

Before Kilpatrick and Hobek undertook the train robbery, however, it is believed that they robbed banks in Oklahoma and one in Elmo, Texas. Kilpatrick also was identified as a suspect in the robbery of railroad stations in the Texas towns of San Antonio and San Diego. It is also supposed that Kilpatrick and Hobek were involved in several instances of horse theft in parts of West Texas. Some sources claim that Kilpatrick's brother, Felix, accompanied him on some of the robberies and the rustling.

During the late evening of March 13, 1912, the Southern Pacific *Sunset Limited* pulled up to a siding at Dryden, Texas, a remote and somewhat isolated and unmanned station in Terrell County. The station was surrounded by a seemingly endless expanse of Trans-Pecos desert sparsely carpeted with cactus, creosote bush, and other low-growing vegetation, so that one could see for miles.

Nearly two hours earlier, the *Sunset Limited* had departed Del Rio, Texas, eighty-five miles to the southeast and on the border with Mexico. It was on its way to the tiny town of Sanderson, some twenty-five miles west of Dryden.

The *Sunset Limited* was pulling a mail car and a baggage car, along with a number of passenger cars. Once the train was halted at the station, one of the crewmen added water to the boiler from a tank perched next to the tracks. As this task was being accomplished, the engineer and fireman conducted an inspection of and did maintenance on the locomotive, a routine always required at such stops. This done, the engineer and fireman climbed back into the cab and made preparations to depart.

Just as the *Sunset Limited* began pulling away, Ben Kilpatrick and Ole Hobek dashed from their hiding place near the station and jumped onto the platform of the baggage car. As the train rolled along, gradually picking up speed, the two bandits made their way up the ladder to the top of the car. They crawled across this one and several others, eventually arriving at the coal tender. From the tender, the two men, having donned masks, jumped into the cab of the locomotive, pointed their revolvers at the engineer, and informed him they were going to rob the train. Kilpatrick ordered the engineer to proceed to the first iron bridge east of Baxter's

Curve and stop the train. Baxter's Curve was located about halfway between Dryden and Sanderson.

Once the train stopped, Kilpatrick told the engineer to uncouple the passenger cars and caboose. The express, mail, and baggage cars were to remain attached to the engine. The train crew was assembled, and Hobek searched each of them for weapons.

Once the cars were uncoupled, Kilpatrick then instructed the engineer to cross the bridge, proceed another half mile down the track, and stop. At this point, two horses, apparently belonging to the robbers, could be seen tied nearby to some brush. The presence of the horses suggested the involvement of a third outlaw who had accompanied Kilpatrick and Hobek to the station and then traveled ahead to meet them at this location.

Once the locomotive and the trailing express, mail, and baggage cars had pulled to a stop for a second time, Kilpatrick assigned Hobek the job of standing guard over the engineer. Kilpatrick jumped from the cab to the ground and made his way down the tracks to the express car. The time was 12:05 a.m.

When Kilpatrick reached the Wells Fargo express car (some accounts say it was the baggage car), the outlaw hammered on the car door and instructed the agent inside to open up. On this particular *Sunset Limited* run, two messengers had been assigned the job of accompanying the packages and money. Following a brief period of hesitation on the part of the reluctant messengers, the door eventually slid open, and Kilpatrick climbed in.

Once inside the express car, Kilpatrick, revolver in hand, faced the messengers, Jake Reagan and David Trousdale. Trousdale was thirty-two years old and had not been in his position long. To Kilpatrick, the two messengers appeared unarmed and quite intimidated by his presence. After being threatened by Kilpatrick, who was waving his revolver, the two agents retreated to one end of the car. Kilpatrick immediately went about the task of rummaging through the canvas bags in search of currency and paid little attention to the messengers.

Kilpatrick stuffed a canvas bag with approximately $60,000 in currency and coin and was preparing to leave when Trousdale stepped forward and pointed to a small box on the floor of the car. He told the outlaw that he was under the impression that it contained something of great value. Intrigued, Kilpatrick bent over to examine the box. With the bandit's attention diverted, Trousdale picked up a heavy mallet used to break thick ice. Without hesitating, the messenger swung the mallet and connected with the back of Kilpatrick's head. The outlaw dropped to the floor, moaned, and attempted to rise. Trousdale viciously attacked the outlaw with the mallet, beating him across the head at least a dozen more times. By the time he stopped, Kilpatrick was dead. His skull had been crushed, his neck broken, and his brains splattered on the floor and part of one wall of the express car.

It soon became apparent to Trousdale and Reagan that at least one more train robber was nearby and would no doubt come to the baggage car to check on his partner. In anticipation of such, Trousdale picked up Kilpatrick's rifle, selected a strategic hiding place inside the car, and awaited the arrival of the second man.

Ole Hobek was not long in coming. Trousdale heard the crunch of boots approaching on the railroad gravel outside and realized the man was heading for the express car. A moment later, Hobek was climbing through the open door. Once inside, the robber rose to his full height and looked around the interior of the car. From his hiding place, Trousdale calmly raised the rifle, aimed, and shot. The bullet struck Hobek an inch above the left eye, killing him instantly.

According to one written account, a third outlaw had arrived at the locomotive on horseback and was leading two additional mounts. When he heard the shot fired by the messenger, he spurred his horse and fled. This incident has never been verified; nor has the rider ever been identified.

Moments later, the engineer was apprised of what had happened. When he was certain the two train robbers no longer posed a threat, he backed the locomotive up, recoupled the passenger cars, and continued on toward Sanderson.

When the *Sunset Limited* arrived at the Sanderson station, the engineer alerted the authorities to what had taken place at Baxter's Curve and informed them that the bodies of the two would-be train robbers were in the baggage car. With assistance from agent Trousdale, several lawmen carried the corpses from the car and laid them down on the station platform. It was noted that the two robbers carried a total of six guns.

The bodies of Kilpatrick and Hobek were hoisted from the platform and held upright as several photographs were taken of the dead men. Both were wrapped in sheets, placed in a single coffin, and buried in the Cedar Grove Cemetery in Sanderson.

Thanks to the quick and decisive action of express messenger Trousdale, the contents of the express cars remained safe. Trousdale was pronounced a hero for his efforts at thwarting the robbery of the *Sunset Limited* and lauded by newspapers. As the train was delayed for a time at the Sanderson station, money was collected from the passengers and presented to Trousdale as a reward in gratitude for his bravery, a total of $51.

Later, Wells Fargo presented Trousdale with a $1,000 check. In addition, he received another $1,000 from the US government, and the Southern Pacific Railroad gave him $500. He was also awarded a gold watch. The watch was engraved as follows:

> In recognition of the courage and fidelity displayed
> in an attempted train robbery near Dryden, Texas,
> March 13, 1912, Wells Fargo and Co.

Some newspapers referred to the event as the "Sanderson Train Robbery." Others called it the "Baxter's Curve Train Robbery," and there is at least one reference to the "Dryden Train Robbery."

Due to the efforts of express messenger Trousdale, Ben Kilpatrick, the Tall Texan, one of the most notorious and wanted outlaws and among the most famous train robbers in the history of the American West, would rob no more trains.

Ben Kilpatrick had finally met his end. Coincident with his death, the train robbery era in Texas and the rest of the country was winding down.

CHAPTER 32

WILLIS NEWTON

Willis Newton was born on January 19, 1889, in Cottonwood, Texas, a tiny community forty-five miles southeast of Abilene in Callahan County. Willis was the sixth of eleven children of Jim and Janetta Pecos Newton. As he was growing up, his family had little in the way of possessions or money and knew nothing but hard work in the cotton fields. Following a pattern established by other Texas-related train robbers, Willis escaped his humble beginnings and went on to become the leader of the most successful gang of train robbers in the history of the United States.

Jim Newton was an itinerant farmer and sharecropper for much of his life and secured employment wherever he could find it. This often meant moving from place to place. In 1903, the family, with the children and all their belongings packed into a wagon pulled by two horses, moved back to Cottonwood but did not stay for long. Over the years, the Newtons traveled to and lived in Cisco, Fort Worth, Abilene, Big Spring, and Uvalde. In each location, Jim found work, if only for a few months.

Willis Newton, along with his siblings, knew little but strenuous labor in the cotton fields from dawn until past sundown. Willis was a hard worker, and as he grew into his teens he was lean, hard, and tough. His nickname was "Skinny." Though a competent field hand, Willis was convinced there were better ways to make a living.

As a youth, Willis often left home in search of adventure and other work. He was particularly attracted to trains and soon discovered that it was easy to climb into an empty boxcar or ride the blinds to whatever destination he had selected. Sometimes he was caught and thrown off the train, and he soon grew adept at avoiding the conductors and guards. In time, Willis grew quite familiar with trains, with railroad schedules, and with the responsibilities of the railroad employees.

During his travels, Willis often found himself in trouble with the law, some of it related to illegally riding the trains and some related to theft. Willis found it easy to break into stores and take

Willis Newton

clothes and shoes. More often than not he was adept in evading arrest, but it was just a matter of time before he was caught. In 1909, Willis was arrested for stealing a wagonload of cotton. He was tried, found guilty, and sent to the state penitentiary in Huntsville to serve a term of two years. After a few weeks at Huntsville, he was transferred to another prison in Rusk, where he was joined by his brother Wylie, aka Doc, who was also sentenced to serve a term for theft.

After serving eleven months of his sentence, Willis, along with Doc, escaped. A day later, while on the run, the two fugitives broke into a store and stole some clothes, then fled on foot. Guards and trackers from the prison set off in pursuit of the brothers and caught up with them several days later, rearrested them, and returned them to prison. Willis was sent to the penitentiary at Sugarland, where he served thirty months. As a result of written pleas from his mother, Willis was eventually pardoned by Texas governor O. B. Colquitt.

After leaving prison, Willis continued to find himself in and out of trouble. He eventually returned to Uvalde, where he found work in the cotton fields, but all the while he had his sights set on bigger things. He wondered what it would be like to rob a train.

In 1914 Willis Newton found himself in Cisco, Texas. Once again, he secured employment in the cotton fields. One afternoon while in town, he ran into an old friend, Red Johnson, whom he had known for fifteen years. Between his wages from picking cotton and what he made from gambling, Willis had accumulated $85. Feeling flush, he and Johnson quit the cotton fields and hung around town playing poker and shooting dice. By the time two weeks had passed, both men were out of money. While wondering what to do next, Willis told Johnson that he had been thinking about robbing a train and wondered if Johnson wanted to join him.

Willis knew exactly which train he wanted to rob and the precise location for the heist. The Southern Pacific always stopped for maintenance and inspection at Cline, Texas, a tiny settlement not far from Uvalde. It was to be the introduction to train robbery of a man who would become the best and most successful at this criminal activity there ever was. Although he never garnered the headlines and notoriety devoted to Butch Cassidy, Jesse James, and others, he, along with his gang, was to outshine them all.

CHAPTER 33

CLINE, TEXAS

December 30, 1914

From Cisco, Willis Newton and Red Johnson made their way to the small town of Sabinal. Willis carried a Colt .45 single-action revolver, a weapon he had acquired for $10 several months earlier in Fort Worth. While in Sabinal, the two men were wandering around the town's wagon yard when Johnson spotted a .30-.30 Winchester rifle in the back of a wagon. Johnson grabbed it, and the two ran away. Now, both men were armed.

From Sabinal, they traveled to Uvalde, twenty-two miles to the southwest. Once in town, Willis decided he wanted a .30-.30 Winchester also. One night, the two friends kicked in the door of a store and took a brand-new rifle along with several boxes of shells. This done, they walked to the railroad depot where the westbound Southern Pacific passenger train traveling on the Galveston, Harrisburg, and San Antonio Railway had pulled into the station. Newton knew that after the train departed Uvalde, it traveled to the station at Cline twenty-two miles to the west. He decided that he and Johnson would board the train at Uvalde and ride it to Cline, where they would rob it.

After Willis checked the station schedule and learned that the train would depart the Uvalde station at 11:00 p.m., he discovered that the shells he had taken from the store would not fit the Winchester. He and Johnson raced back to the establishment, broke in again, and exchanged the shells for the correct ones. By the time they returned to the station, the train had already pulled out and was at least a mile down the tracks.

Willis remained convinced that Cline would be the ideal location to rob the train, so having no other means of travel, they set out on foot. Their intention was to wait for the next westbound Southern Pacific to pull into the Cline station, where they would board it and hold it up.

The weather was cold. Newton and Johnson both wore heavy black overcoats and slept out in the open. Along the way, they burglarized a house where Red obtained a newer pair of boots. Three days later, they arrived at the Cline station and learned that the train normally stopped there at 11:30 p.m. The two men waited in the shadows behind the freight house.

Right on time, the Southern Pacific pulled into the station. As the locomotive idled, one of the train crew added water to the boiler from a large tank nearby. The engineer, along with another crewman, busied himself with performing the routine inspection and maintenance required at such stops. Though the train did not linger long at these somewhat remote stations, passengers were free to exit the car and stroll around the station for a few minutes.

When the engineer signaled that the time to leave was approaching, the handful of passengers taking a break on the station dock ambled back into the cars.

In hiding, Newton and Johnson pulled the linings out of their overcoats to fashion masks.

Moments later, as the train was preparing to pull away from the station, Newton and Johnson emerged from behind the freight house, ran toward the last car, and climbed aboard the rear sleeping coach. They were immediately confronted by the brakeman, who ordered them off the train, but when Newton jammed his revolver into the man's belly, he provided no more resistance.

Newton located the porter and, at gunpoint, ordered him to awaken the passengers. As soon as the travelers left their berths, they were approached by the bandits, who demanded their money and valuables. The frightened passengers complied. One of the first to be robbed was a man named Watkins, who happened to be the superintendent of the Southern Pacific Railroad.

All the men were robbed. If a man and woman were together, both were robbed, but single women were left alone. The robbery took place in a matter of a few minutes, and the passengers were sent back to their berths. Hours later, when the train stopped at Spofford in southern Kinney County, the two robbers jumped off and fled the scene on foot.

Newton and Johnson missed an opportunity to harvest even more money from the passengers. During the robbery, they ignored the drawing rooms of the sleeper cars. It was reported that one of them was occupied by a wealthy Mexican citizen who was traveling with over $10,000 in money and $15,000 worth of jewelry. The robbers escaped with just over $4,700.

Newton and Johnson fled on foot, eventually arriving at Crystal City fifty-five miles to the southeast, where Willis's mother lived.

If an organized search for and pursuit of the robbers was ever undertaken, there is no record of it, and their identities remained a complete mystery for another half century. For years, searches for specific details relating to the Cline train robbery led to dead ends. Newspaper reporting of the crime was practically nonexistent, and a search of the records of the Southern Pacific Railroad yielded no information whatsoever.

The specific details of the Cline train robbery eventually came from Willis Newton himself over a half century later. During an interview, he admitted his role in the affair, identified his partner as Red Johnson, and stated that it was his first train robbery.

Newton went on to enjoy an amazing and successful career as a bank and train robber. For the first few years, his gang

consisted of individuals who came and went, but in time he recruited his brothers—Jess, Doc, and Joe—along with a man named
Brentwood Glasscock. This gang became the most successful bank
and train robbery team in the history of the United States. With
Willis Newton as the leader and planner, the gang was responsible
for robbing eighty banks. Most of the bank robberies were in Texas
and Colorado, with some as far east as Arkansas and as far north
as Canada. Following the successful Cline train robbery, Willis
engineered another five.

CHAPTER 34

BROWNSVILLE, TEXAS

October 18, 1915

The stopping and robbery of a St. Louis, Brownsville, and Mexico (StLB&M) train six and a half miles north of Brownsville on October 18, 1915, represented a dramatic departure from the pattern of Texas train robberies that citizens had grown accustomed to. Unlike previous robberies in the Lone Star State, which had been conducted by homegrown outlaws, this one was undertaken for the most part by a band of Mexican nationals whose identities have been disputed, and the reasons for the robbery were largely undetermined.

In broad daylight, a large band of Mexican raiders, some on horseback and some on foot, crossed the Rio Grande in South Texas near Brownsville and traveled to a point known as Tandy's Crossing. The crossing was located near a trestle three miles north of the better-known Olmito Crossing. Estimates of the number of raiders who traveled to Tandy's Crossing ranges from fifty to more than one hundred. Some researchers also believe that the raiders were joined by a number of Mexican citizens who were living and working north of the border.

A few writers are convinced that the raiders were led by a man named Aniceto Pizano, though this has never been determined for certain. Pizano in fact owned and operated a large ranch on the Texas side of the border. On finally making their way down to Olmito Crossing, the raiders, presumably instructed by Pizano, occupied themselves with preparations to derail the StLB&M train when it passed through several hours later.

J. L. Allahands, who lived a short distance from Olmito Crossing, stated that the raiders removed the spikes and angle bars from a rail on the west side of the tracks. From hiding, Allahands watched as the raiders fastened a stout wire to the rail, stretched it about twenty feet from the tracks, and tied it fast to a shovel handle. When all the preparations had been made, the raiders hid in the nearby brush and arroyos and waited for the arrival of the train.

An hour passed, and the StLB&M train could be heard from a distance. Moments later, it was spotted coming down the track toward the trestle. At the time, it was traveling at thirty-five miles per hour. Seconds before the locomotive reached the point where the rail had been tampered with, three of the raiders pulled hard on the shovel, which in turn caused the rail to be pulled aside. When the locomotive reached the detached rail, it jumped the track, bounced along the wooden ties, and was eventually thrown at a right angle to the direction of the tracks, where it turned over. When the locomotive fell on its side, the engineer was killed and the fireman badly injured. Behind the locomotive, the mail car and baggage car likewise toppled over onto their sides.

Seconds later, when the entire train finally stopped, the raiders rose up from their hiding places and began firing rifles and revolvers, the bullets peppering the passenger coaches. Windows were shattered, and commuters were sprayed with broken glass. This done, the raiders slowly advanced on the train. Most of them headed toward two particular coaches that were carrying a number of soldiers, along with Anglo, black, and Mexican travelers. It was as if the bandits had specifically identified these cars as their targets well in advance of the derailment.

Several raiders entered the first of the coaches. As they poured into the car, they waved their weapons, shouted curses, and threatened the travelers as they made their way along the aisle. Frightened passengers screamed while others begged for mercy. One passenger who attempted to hide between the seats was shot.

Dr. Edgar S. McCain (sometimes reported as Dr. Eugene Shannon McCain) and a former Texas Ranger named H. J. Wallace dashed for what they presumed was the safety of the bathroom located at one end of the car. They were followed close behind by a teenage Mexican boy, also a passenger. After the three had locked themselves in the lavatory, the raiders beat on the door with the butts of their rifles and ordered them to come out. When the door was finally opened, one of the raiders grabbed the Mexican youth and yanked him out of the bathroom. Two other raiders standing nearby fired into the small latrine, one of the bullets striking Wallace in the shoulder. A moment later, McCain was struck in the abdomen, receiving a wound that proved fatal.

By this time the second passenger car had been invaded. The raiders ran through both coaches yelling, "Matan los soldados y los Americanos cabrones!" (Kill the soldiers and the American bastards!). During the ensuing excitement, three soldiers were shot dead and five more wounded. Anglos and blacks were robbed of cash, watches, jewelry, and whatever they carried in their suitcases that appealed to the bandits. All the Mexican passengers were spared, and none of their valuables were taken.

When the raiders finished their depredations of the two passenger coaches, they quickly departed. After leaving the cars, they fled into the nearby brush and arroyos where their horses were tethered and made their getaway. During their flight, they set fire to the railroad trestle. The robbery had been well planned; it was carried out effectively and efficiently, a significant amount of money and jewelry was harvested, and as far as is known not a single raider was injured.

The following day, the newspapers reported the episode and referred to it as the "Brownsville Train Robbery." Few had ever heard of Olmito Crossing, and most of those who had didn't know where it was. It was described as "the boldest raid yet by Mexicans into United States Territory." This was quite a statement considering that there had been a number of cross-border incursions during the preceding twenty years wherein dozens of people had been killed.

Though speculation was rampant, no one has determined to this day whether the bandits were affiliated with the Mexican military. Initially the notion was advanced that at least some of the raiders were members of the Mexican army, and it was written that a few of them were wearing military uniforms. It was also reported that several of the bandits passing through the passenger coaches were shouting, "Viva Carranza!" The actual extent, if any, of the involvement of Mexican general Venustiano Carranza's troops in this, as well as other border raids, has never been verified.

It must be remembered that during this time the Mexican Revolution had been raging, and cross-border raids were common. In many cases, raiders came from Mexico hoping to procure arms and ammunition from whatever source they could determine.

Others dismissed the notion that the raiders were associated with the Mexican army, insisting that they were simply outlaws operating on their own. With regard to the military uniforms worn by a few, some reasoned that it was not uncommon for peasants to appropriate discarded uniforms.

US Army general Frederick Funston assumed the position that Emiliano P. Navarette, the mayor of Matamoros, across the river from Brownsville, had instigated and perhaps even organized the attack on the train. Funston's reasons for his suspicions and accusation were never clear, and though requests were made, he never advanced any evidence supporting his claim. Some have suspected Funston of manufacturing a reason to organize a military contingent to invade Matamoros.

Following reports of what some of the newspapers called the "Brownsville Train Robbery" and the "Olmito Train Robbery," along with the descriptions of the shooting and other violence, Texas residents in the Brownsville area grew fearful of additional raids from across the border and demanded protection from the US military.

A great many citizens clamored for retribution following the raid. Tensions between American citizens and Mexicans, as well as Mexicans residing in Texas, were already high, and violence was not uncommon. Newspapers were filled with demands relating to eradicating any and all Mexicans, referring to them as "mangy wolves," "lice in the thickets," and "hounds of perdition," all hateful references to the Mexican American residents of the region.

Most of the Mexicans living and working on the Texas side of the border were decent, honest, and hardworking and caused little to no trouble for area law enforcement. They went about their lives without complaint and generally minded their own business. Despite this, intense racism festered throughout the area, frustrations exploded into additional violence, and a number of innocent Mexicans were slain.

In one case, a deputy sheriff led a posse of armed and vengeance-minded riders into a field where Mexican laborers were harvesting a crop. The lawmen shot and killed eleven of them for no reason other than that they were "foreigners." An investigation later determined that none of the slain men had been connected to the train robbery in any way.

Several days later, six additional Mexicans were "suspected" of being involved with the robbery. They were pursued and gunned down. As with the previous incident, it was later determined that none of them had anything to do with the Brownsville robbery whatsoever.

In another case, a platoon of Texas Rangers, men with murder in their hearts, rode down four Mexicans they encountered on a road and hung them from a nearby tree. The leader of the Ranger contingent explained that the lynching was intended to serve as an example to any Mexicans living in the area.

Other Mexican residents in the Brownsville region were subjected to ongoing harassment in the period following the train robbery. Several were arrested on spurious charges and held for trial. Because of the aggressive and overtly racist attitudes of the Texas Rangers, as well as others appointed to serve the law, relations between the Anglo and Mexican communities along the Rio Grande deteriorated markedly and remained contentious for years, which caused numerous hostilities following the Brownsville Train Robbery.

Over the years a number of explanations were advanced for the motives behind the Brownsville Train Robbery. Dr. Rodolfo Rocha, a professor of history at the University of Texas, Edinburg, and an authority on Rio Grande valley goings-on during the early 1900s, insisted that the train robbery, as well as other outlawry taking place in South Texas during this time, was a form of social protest against injustices committed against Mexican American citizens. Most of these injustices, according to the record, were perpetrated by elected and appointed law enforcement authorities and the Texas Rangers.

Others have suggested that the motivation for the Brownsville train incident was purely robbery—nothing more, nothing less. Still others cling to the notion that the bandits were Carranzistas, who were accumulating money to purchase arms and ammunition for the ongoing Mexican Revolution.

Dr. Rocha referred to the Brownsville train robbers as "social bandits." He claimed that the robbery was little more than a "spillover from the Mexican Revolution" and that the raiders, frustrated with the social conditions in the Rio Grande valley, were "influenced by the ideology of the . . . Revolution, which was the movement of landless peasants." Rocha pointed out that many of the Mexican American citizens living in the Rio Grande valley had long been subjected to intense abuse by Anglos.

In the end, none of the Brownsville train robbers were ever apprehended or even positively identified. Despite academic proclamations by such as Dr. Rocha, no one has ever agreed on a motive for the robbery. Further, any affiliations the bandits may have had with military or other entities have never been proven.

As tensions rose following the Brownsville Train Robbery, anticipation of another attack pervaded area Anglo communities. Fear and paranoia were common, and years passed before things settled down in the region. While additional cross-border raids took place up and down the Rio Grande valley, no more area train robberies occurred, much to the relief of the railroads and citizens alike.

CHAPTER 35

BELLS, TEXAS
August 25, 1921

In 1921, Bells was a tiny community located fifteen miles south of Denison. Veteran train and bank robber Willis Newton began to focus on this location for his next heist.

By the spring of 1921, Willis had recruited three of his brothers into his gang: Joe, Doc, and Jess. They were joined by Brentwood Glasscock. Glasscock had been a member of the gang previously, left, and then come back. According to Willis, Glasscock "wasn't fit for nothing, just only to drive the car. He knowed all about a car and was a good driver."

The days of employing horses for train robberies and escapes was now long past. Willis was partial to Studebakers and began using them regularly for his robberies, both bank and train. He preferred the Studebaker "Big Six" and the "Special Six." Willis claimed they were the best road cars of the day, that they were "tough," and that "you could just run them into anything."

Invariably, the Studebakers used by the gang were stolen a day or two before a robbery. They would be driven until the tread on the tires was worn down, discarded, and new tires were appropriated.

Accompanied by brother Jess and Glasscock, Willis traveled from where they were living at the time in Tulsa, Oklahoma, down to Glenwood, Texas, where there was a transfer station for the Katy (officially, the Missouri-Kansas-Texas) Railroad. As they watched from hiding, the gang members observed several large sacks being lifted into the mail car. The sacks were made of heavy canvas and when filled assumed a square shape and were secured at the top with a big brass lock. These were the types of sacks used by the Federal Reserve Bank and other banks to ship currency. Willis discovered that similar sacks were loaded into a mail car every night. He assumed that each of the sacks contained a lot of money.

Willis also learned that the train stopped at the small town of Bells. The three men traveled here. Willis explained that he and Glasscock would enter the mail car and, after the train had traveled a short distance, throw the mail bags out. When the train slowed down on arriving at Denison, Willis and Glasscock planned to jump from the train and make their way back down the tracks to the loot, where they would be met by Jess in one of the Studebakers.

On the night of the robbery, the weather was warm and the doors to the mail car left open. As the train pulled out, Willis and Glasscock ran out of hiding and jumped into the car. They were immediately confronted by the mail clerk, who reached for his revolver. He wasn't fast enough; before he could pull his weapon from the holster, Willis had his own revolver out and pointed at the man's chest. As he took the clerk's weapon away, he noticed a second clerk lurking in the shadows of the car in the process of drawing his revolver. Willis likewise disarmed him and made the two men lie face down on the floor of the car. Yet a third clerk made his presence known and a moment later was lying next to the others.

At that point, Willis noticed that Glasscock had withdrawn to the opening of the mail car, afraid to come inside. Years later when interviewed, Willis referred to Glasscock as a "dirty louse" and a "dirty coward" and ordered him to come inside the mail car. Once inside the car and seeing the three clerks disarmed and lying on the floor, Glasscock's courage returned, and he began acting tough, striking and kicking the defenseless clerks.

Somehow, Willis got the train stopped, and he and Glasscock threw the sacks onto the ground. Within a couple of hours, brother Jess arrived in one of the Studebakers. The sacks were loaded into the trunk, and moments later the robbers made their escape. Afterward, when they stopped long enough to open the sacks and count the money, they discovered that they had only come away with a few thousand dollars. Willis later learned that this was a smaller, secondary shipment of currency and that the larger one had occurred the day before.

What has been referred to as the Bells train robbery received very little attention, and coverage by newspapers was nonexistent. Because the amount of money stolen was relatively small, and because the identity of the robbers was not known or even suspected, the matter was soon dropped.

As with the Cline train robbery of December 30, 1914, specific details of the Bells robbery eluded investigators until Willis Newton was interviewed during the 1970s, revealing who was involved and the modus operandi. By then, Willis and his brothers were old men, had spent considerable time in prison, and had either served their appropriate sentences or outlived the statute of limitations for all their train and bank robberies.

CHAPTER 36

BLOOMBERG, TEXAS

Uncertain, 1921

Disappointed with the amount of money taken from the Bells robbery, Willis Newton wasted no time in planning another heist. While hiding out in Texarkana, the gang would walk down to the depot and scrutinize the activity there. They noticed that once each week, when the train arrived from Shreveport, a man would climb out of the express car carrying a big black box, which he deposited at the express office. Willis learned that the black box contained currency.

Willis studied the situation and in the process learned the route of the Shreveport train. In the end, he decided the greatest potential for stealing the big black box full of money would be when the train stopped at Bloomberg, Texas, twenty miles to the south.

Willis, Doc, and Jess Newton, along with Brentwood Glasscock, traveled to Bloomberg, located the train station, and found a convenient hiding place in the nearby woods. After determining the location where they would stop the train and rob it, they made arrangements for brother Joe to pick them up.

The Newton brothers and Glasscock watched from hiding as the train took on water, inspections were conducted, and passengers lolled around the platform visiting and smoking. It was 10:00 p.m. Moments later, when all was ready, the conductor gave the signal to depart. Just as the train pulled away from the Bloomberg station, the four robbers ran from hiding and jumped onto the blinds.

Wylie "Doc" Newton

Joe Newton

Jess Newton

As the train approached the Sulphur River Bridge ten miles to the north, Willis and Jess made their way over the tops of the cars and the tender and into the locomotive cab where they waved their revolvers at the engineer and fireman. Once he had their attention, Willis told the engineer to start slowing down as they approached the bridge. He further instructed the frightened man to stop the train when the mail car was just off the north side of the bridge and the rest of the cars were positioned on the structure.

Willis climbed back on top and ran back to the mail car. Near the middle of the car was a vent that had been cranked open to get fresh air into the car. Willis pulled a bottle of formaldehyde from a pocket, uncorked it, and dumped the contents into the car. At the same time, he yelled into the opening that it was poison and ordered the clerks to slide open the car door. The smell of the formaldehyde frightened the clerks, and they rushed to open the doors and scramble out of the car.

Willis located a porter and ordered him to uncouple the mail car from the trailing ones. This done, he ordered the porter into the mail car and asked him about the location of the big black box. The porter explained that the box had not been delivered to the car on this night. Disappointed at not acquiring the box, Willis hunted throughout the car and found three sacks of registered mail.

Willis hurried back to the locomotive and instructed the engineer to move the train on up the tracks, leaving the passenger coaches behind on the bridge. On arriving at Texarkana, the gang of robbers took the mail sacks, left the train, and instructed the engineer to head back to the Sulphur River Bridge and hook up the cars that had been left there. This done, the gang ran into the woods to a predetermined location where they were picked up by brother Joe.

According to Willis Newton, after opening the mail sacks, they found "a bunch of bonds and stuff," some of which were converted into money.

As with the Cline and Bells train robberies, information on this episode was scarce until Willis Newton revealed the details of the heist during the 1970s.

At the completion of the Bloomberg train robbery, Willis Newton and his gang, dubbed the Newton Boys, were now practiced and confident. They went on to rob more trains and banks. Their career reached an apex shortly after they pulled off the greatest train robbery in US history at Rondout, Illinois, in 1924.

CHAPTER 37

THE END OF THE NEWTON BROTHERS GANG

According to train robbery historians, the largest heist ever pulled off took place on June 12, 1924, near Rondout, Illinois, a railroad junction located thirty miles north of Chicago. Close to $3 million (some reports claim $4 million) worth of currency and bonds from the Federal Reserve Bank of Chicago that were being shipped to banks in the northeastern part of the United States were taken. The robbery was planned and executed primarily by Willis Newton from Uvalde, Texas, who was accompanied by brothers Doc, Jess, and Joe Newton and accomplice Brentwood Glasscock.

The Newton brothers were not only successful train and bank robbers but colorful and adventurous characters who easily slid into lives of crime, regarding such as far more profitable and fun than working on a farm. The foursome, inspired in large part by Willis, approached the business of robbing trains and banks the same as anyone committed to any other profession. And they were good at it, becoming regarded as the most successful bank robbers in the history of the United States. The truth is, they also had fun. During their later years, Willis and Joe Newton were interviewed for a documentary. As they related their adventures as train and bank robbers during the early 1920s, the two men smiled, and it was clear they were proud of their accomplishments. The truth is, they never felt more alive than when robbing a train or bank.

Like a number of other Texas train robbers over the years, the Newton brothers were raised in a farm family. Not content to labor in the cotton fields all day, the brothers were eager for other opportunities. Between 1914 and 1924, the gang robbed trains and banks. Joe Newton estimated that over the years the brothers stole well over $4 million, more than "all the famous bank and train robbers put together," including Jesse James, Butch Cassidy, Sam Bass, and Black Jack Ketchum.

Willis was the first of the brothers to engage in crime, and the others followed a short time later. In 1909, he and Doc were arrested for stealing cotton and for vagrancy and were sentenced to two years each in a Texas penitentiary. Both escaped but were recaptured and sentenced to serve more time. Texas governor O. B. Colquitt later pardoned both young men. It was later learned from Willis Newton that Colquitt was susceptible to bribery and that during his term as governor he released a number of prisoners in exchange for under-the-table payments.

Prison provided no lessons at all for Willis, other than causing him to become more determined than before to engage in crime. Thus far, his entire life had been little more than poverty and back-breaking farm labor. He also maintained that he had been wrongly charged in some instances and unjustly imprisoned. When released from confinement, he was, according to one writer, determined to "become the outlaw that the authorities envisioned him to be."

Following his first train robbery in 1914, Willis found other outlets for his penchant for stealing. In 1917 he was arrested on a charge of bank robbery in Marble Falls, Texas, but released a short time later. Without allowing much time to pass, Willis turned to petty theft and gambling. He was arrested again and sent to the penitentiary but served less than a year before he was pardoned once again, this time by Governor William P. Hobby.

Gathering about him a small gang around this time (not his brothers), Willis robbed stores in Mineral Wells, Denton, and

Abilene, Texas. They stole money, clothing, tools, and shoes. In Winters, Texas, Willis and his team robbed $3,500 worth of Liberty Bonds from a bank. During pursuit by law enforcement authorities, one of the gang members was shot and killed. Wasting no time at all, the gang went on to rob banks and stores in Texas, Oklahoma, Kansas, and Michigan.

In 1920, brother Joe quit his job breaking horses on a ranch near Uvalde and joined Willis. The two brothers, along with Brentwood Glasscock (at least one writer gives his name as Joe Glasscock), robbed banks in Nebraska and Iowa. Joe Newton was only nineteen years old at the time.

In 1921, Willis talked brothers Doc and Jess into joining the gang. Willis was the oldest and most experienced of the four brothers and thus assumed the mantle of leader. For the most part the brothers concentrated on robbing banks but, according to Joe, mixed in "an occasional train holdup for the fun of it and for the booty that usually rode in the baggage and mail cars."

The well-established gang of four brothers, along with Glasscock and occasionally some others, went on to rob banks and trains throughout Texas, Missouri, Indiana, South Dakota, and Arkansas and in Canada. During their decade-long career as bank and train robbers, the Newton brothers appeared to be enjoying themselves at every turn. In 1976, Willis Newton was quoted as saying, "We never killed anybody and we never wanted to. All we wanted was the money. . . . Robbing banks and trains was our way of getting it. That was our business."

According to Joe, he and his brothers held up more than eighty banks. He also claimed that they robbed a total of six trains. Joe agreed with Willis that in the process of committing all these robberies, they never killed anybody, but it was not for lack of trying. The truth is, members of the gang are on record as having shot and wounded several victims.

Most of the robberies committed by the gang known as the Newton Boys were in Texas and Colorado, but the bandits ventured far and wide. The only robbery they committed east of the Mississippi River, as far as is known, was the train holdup in Rondout, Illinois. It was to be their last.

When the Newton brothers began their crime spree, the most common mode of travel was by horseback. By the time the 1920s arrived, the siblings had greater access to automobiles, which they found to be more efficient and faster than horses. Early on, the brothers preferred Studebakers but later graduated to Cadillacs. In fact, they used a Cadillac in the Rondout train robbery.

Willis, Jess, and Doc Newton climbed aboard the tender of the Chicago, Milwaukee, and St. Paul mail train just before it departed the station. Joe Newton and Brentwood Glasscock were waiting nearby in the Cadillac. Moments later, the trio of robbers dropped into the cab of the locomotive, took control from the engineer, and set the air brakes. This accomplished, they dropped to the ground and headed toward the mail car. Within seconds after forcing open the door to the car, they were fired upon by the mail clerks and guards stationed inside.

Willis was prepared for such resistance. Taking cover from the fusillade, he uncorked a large vial of formaldehyde and tossed the contents into the car through one of the windows. The fumes from the strong liquid temporarily blinded the occupants and rendered them helpless. The Newton Boys subsequently overpowered the guards and relieved them of their weapons. After taking what they wanted from this car, the robbers proceeded to the second and third.

During the robbery, gang member Glasscock panicked and accidentally shot Doc five times. After escaping, the gang hid out not far from the robbery site and decided to lay low while waiting for Doc to recover from his wounds. It wasn't long, however, before lawmen caught up with them. They were arrested, tried, and sentenced to the penitentiary at Leavenworth, Kansas. Doc served six years, Willis served four, Joe served one, and Jess served nine months.

During the investigation of the train robbery, authorities learned that a high-ranking Chicago postal inspector had worked closely with the Newton brothers in planning the heist. The inspector likewise was arrested and spent ten years in prison for his participation in the robbery.

Following his release from prison, Willis returned to Uvalde, a town that by this time he and his brothers regarded as home. He was forty years old. Willis had spent much of his time as a train and bank robber on the road traveling from one town to another, rarely returning to Uvalde, where he had a home and a wife, Louise.

Willis found occasional work on area ranches and doing odd jobs. At one point, he was seduced by the prospect of making some easy money by hauling contraband whiskey. This proved profitable for a while, but he eventually got caught and sent back to Leavenworth for a time. Willis Newton passed away on August 22, 1979, at the age of ninety.

After Jess was released from prison, he returned to Texas and attempted to live a quiet life. By all accounts, he succeeded. He worked on ranches near Uvalde until he grew too old and infirm. He eschewed publicity of any kind, and while Willis and Joe never hesitated to relate their train- and bank-robbing adventures to reporters and tourists, Jess kept to himself. He died of lung cancer in 1960 at age seventy-three.

Willis and Joe were apprehended as suspects in a bank robbery in Oklahoma in 1932. Until his dying day, however, Joe insisted that neither he nor Willis were the robbers. Despite their protestations of innocence, both men were sentenced to another ten years in prison. Willis served four years, and Joe served one.

Doc Newton apparently had not had enough excitement to get him through his later years. He found work on farms in Oklahoma and Missouri for a time, occasionally taking a break from these labors to run whiskey. In 1968, at the age of seventy-seven, Doc decided he wanted to rob another bank. One night he broke into the bank at Rowena, a tiny town in Runnels County in central Texas. Oddly, the bank had no alarm, but the one in the liquor store next door was set off, and lawmen arrived a short time later. Apparently deciding he had nothing to lose, Doc chose to shoot it out with the police. He was unsuccessful and eventually subdued and arrested. During the melee, Doc was struck in the head, suffering an injury that resulted in brain damage that was to affect him for the rest of his life.

At the end of Doc's trial, he was found guilty and sentenced to two years in prison. The crime called for significantly more jail time, but the judge felt that some level of leniency was in order because of Doc's advanced age. Doc was shipped to the prison hospital at Fort Stockton, Texas, where he served out his full sentence. He spent most of his prison time in the infirmary. After being released, Doc returned to Uvalde, where he died of cancer in 1974 at age eighty-three.

Joe Newton likewise returned to Uvalde, took up ranching, and for a time worked in a butcher shop. In 1957, he sold his ranch and purchased a corner lot near the Uvalde town square, where he opened a café and filling station. Joe hung around the businesses and, along with Willis, regaled customers with his train- and bank-robbing exploits.

By 1980, Joe decided running his businesses was more trouble than he could endure, so he retired. From time to time he reveled in the opportunity to tell stories of his outlaw days and enjoyed his reputation as what the newspapers referred to as the "last living train robber."

During the early part of 1980, Trinity University (Texas) students produced a documentary film titled *The Newton Boys: Portrait of an Outlaw Gang*. The film brought more celebrity attention to the brothers, and Joe made an appearance on NBC's *Tonight Show Starring Johnny Carson*.

Joe spent most of his retirement hunting and fishing. He died on February 3, 1989, at the age of eighty-eight.

In 1994, a book was published that also was titled *The Newton Boys: Portrait of an Outlaw Gang*. The authors are listed as Willis and Joe Newton, but the book shared their stories as told to writers Claude Stanush and David Middleton. In 1998, a motion picture called *The Newton Boys*, starring Matthew McConaughey and Ethan Hawke, was released and enjoyed mild success around the country. The film introduced a new generation to the adventures of Willis Newton and his brothers. In 2013 another book, *Willis Newton: The Last Texas Outlaw*, by G. R. Williamson, was released, adding more to the growing layers of Newton brothers' legend and lore.

Without a doubt, the Newton Boys of Texas were the last of America's great train robbers. Following their heist of the Chicago, Milwaukee, and St. Paul at Rondout, Illinois, train robbery in the United States, for the most part, came to an end. Although one more robbery occurred at McAvoy, California, in 1929, it was minor in comparison: the haul amounted to little ($1,600), and the robbers were quickly apprehended, tried, sent to prison, and forgotten.

To this day, the legacy of the Newton Boys of Texas remains intact.

BIBLIOGRAPHY

BOOKS

Anonymous. *Life and Adventures of Sam Bass.* Dallas, TX: Dallas Commercial Steam Print, 1878.

Anonymous (by a Citizen of Denton County, Texas). *Authentic History of Sam Bass and His Gang.* Denton, TX: Monitor Job Office, 1978.

Block, Eugene B. *Great Train Robberies of the West.* New York: Coward-McCann, Inc., 1959.

Breihan, Carl. *Rube Burrow: King of the Train Robbers.* West Allis, WI: Leather Stocking Books, 1981.

Castleman, Harvey N. *Sam Bass, the Train Robber.* Garland, KS: Haldeman-Julius Publications, 1944.

Dillon, Richard. *Wells, Fargo Detective: A Biography of James B. Hume.* Reno: University of Nevada Press, 1986.

Gard, Wayne. *Sam Bass.* Norman: University of Oklahoma Press, 1960.

Harlow, Alvin F. *Old Waybills.* New York: Appleton-Century, 1937.

Hatch, Alden. *American Express: A Century of Service.* Garden City, NY: Doubleday and Company, Inc., 1960.

Hoole, William Stanley. *The Saga of Rube Burrow, King of America's Train Robbers.* Tuscaloosa, AL: Confederate Publishing Company, 1981.

Hungerford, Edward. *Wells Fargo: Advancing the American Frontier.* New York: Random House, 1949.

Nash, Robert. *Encyclopedia of Western Lawmen and Outlaws.* Boston: Da Capo Press, 1994.

Newton, Willis, and Joe Newton (as told to Claude Stanush and David Middleton). *The Newton Boys: Portrait of an Outlaw Gang.* Austin, TX: State House Press, 1994.

O'Neal, Bill. *Encyclopedia of Western Gunfighters.* Norman: University of Oklahoma Press, 1979.

Parsons, Chuck. *Captain John R. Hughes, Lone Star Ranger.* Denton: University of North Texas Press, 2011.

Patterson, Richard. *The Train Robbery Era: An Encyclopedic History.* Boulder, CO: Pruett Publishing Company, 1991.

Shirley, Glenn. *West of Hell's Fringe: Crime, Criminals, and the Federal Peace Officer in Oklahoma Territory.* Norman: University of Oklahoma Press, 1978.

Soule, Arthur. *The Tall Texan: The Story of Ben Kilpatrick.* Deer Lodge, MT: Trail Dust Publishing, Inc., 1996.

Webb, Walter Prescott. *The Texas Rangers: A Century of Frontier Defense.* Austin: University of Texas Press, 1935.

Williamson, G. R. *Willis Newton: The Last Outlaw.* Miami, FL: Old Time Press, 2013.

MAGAZINE ARTICLES

Agee, G. L. "Rube Burrow: King of Outlaws and His Band of Train Robbers." *Old West* (spring 1968).

Maguire, Jack. "The Texas Terrors." *Southwest Airlines Magazine* (August 1984).

McPhaul, John J. "Inside the Great Rondout Train Robbery." *True Detective Mysteries* (April 1930).

Romero, Trancito (as told to R. C. Valdez). "I Saw Black Jack Hanged." *True West* (September–October 1958).

NEWSPAPERS

Birmingham Weekly Age Herald, October 10, 1890 (Birmingham, Alabama).

Deseret Evening News, December 21, 1889.

Galveston News, February 23, 1878 (Galveston, Texas).

New York Times, May 20, 1887; June 29, June 30, and July 2, 1893; October 13, 1897; December 14, 1900; and December 31, 1914 (New York, New York).

Sacramento Daily Union, June 11, 1898 (Sacramento, California).

ACKNOWLEDGMENTS

By the time a book is released, it is the product of the contributions of a team of professionals committed to quality, a team of which the author is proud to be a part. This publication would have never seen the light of day had it not been for the assistance and leadership of some special people.

C. W. Quallenberg was always available and provided valuable advice and direction in all matters relating to computers. I am honored to be able to include the fine illustrations rendered by noted artist Richard "Peewee" Kolb. Heaps of gratitude are extended to my intrepid agent, Sandra Bond, who manages to place nearly every manuscript I send her. The fine editorial eye of Courtney Oppel smoothed out some rough spots and enhanced the quality of this work. Thanks to all of you.

Finally, to Laurie Jameson, oft-published and honored writer and poet who is always my first reader and visionary editor.

INDEX

ABOUT THE AUTHOR

W. C. Jameson is the award-winning author of over one hundred books and hundreds of articles. Several of his books have been optioned for film and television, and he has appeared as an authority on a variety of topics on the History Channel, the Discovery Channel, the Travel Channel, Fox News, PBS, and *Nightline*. A professional treasure hunter for more than five decades, Jameson has served as a consultant on the topic for film and television and has been inducted into the Treasure Hunters Hall of Fame.